EXERCISE SCHOOL FOR
Horse and Rider

EXERCISE SCHOOL FOR
Horse and
Rider

LESLEY SKIPPER

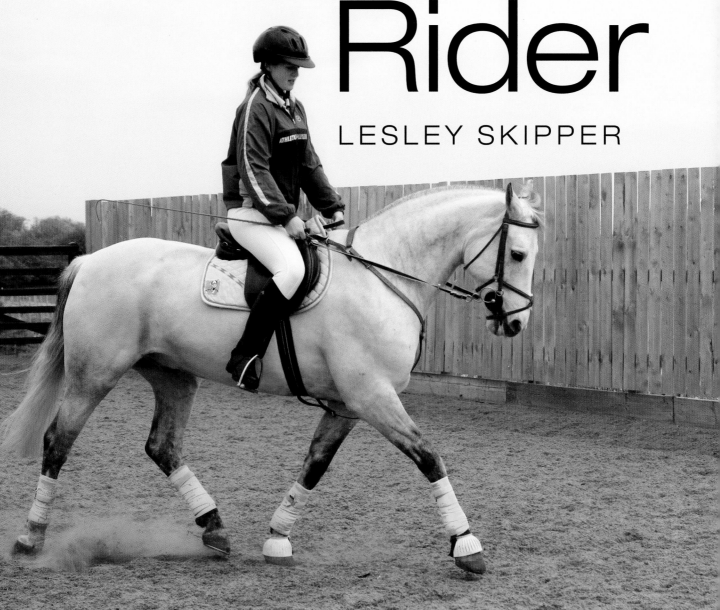

NH
NEW
HOLLAND

First published in 2008 by New Holland Publishers (UK) Ltd
London • Cape Town • Sydney • Auckland
www.newhollandpublishers.com

Garfield House, 86–88
Edgware Road, London
W2 2EA, United Kingdom

Unit 1, 66 Gibbes Street,
Chatswood, NSW 2067,
Australia

80 McKenzie Street, Cape
Town 8001, South Africa

218 Lake Road, Northcote,
Auckland, New Zealand

ISBN 978 1 84773 004 6

Senior Editor: Sarah Goulding
Designer: Stonecastle Graphics Ltd
Illustrator: Maggie Raynor
Production: Marion Storz
Publishing Director: Rosemary Wilkinson

Reproduction by Pica Digital Pte Ltd, Singapore
Printed and bound by Tien Wah Press Pte Ltd, Singapore

Contents

Introduction

IN THE first decade of the twenty-first century we are faced with a bewildering range of horse-training methods. Equestrian magazines carry numerous articles by practitioners of this or that method. Countless websites extol the virtues of X, Y or Z, who may also hold clinics and training courses all over the world. Some of the methods employed are said to incorporate aspects of the horse's natural behaviour, while others consist of cues that the horse has to be taught, usually after some trial and error.

Unfortunately, those who base their methods on equine social behaviour have often taken some aspect of that behaviour out of context, or relied on assumptions that may

not be correct. And those who teach an elaborate system of learned cues have usually ignored the most important aspect of training the ridden horse: the physical interaction of horse and rider. In spite of the undoubted success of individual trainers, very often the only way that they can get their students and followers to reproduce something like that success is by instructing them to follow the method exactly.

Above: *Many people think of classical riding in terms of the Baroque horses of Portugal and Spain. Here, Don Francisco de Bragança is riding Sylvia Loch's Lusitano mare Queijada.*

Left: *Horses are not machines, but individuals – living creatures with their own thoughts, emotions and priorities. Sylvia Loch's Lusitano x TB gelding Espada is a noble horse with a very decided personality!*

Veterinary surgeon Sara Wyche, who has studied the horse–rider interaction in depth, says that:

> … there are two ways of learning any subject. It doesn't matter whether it's an intellectual subject, such as a science or a language, or a manual skill, such as operating a machine or playing a game. The first way is to learn hundreds of instructions, and follow them. The second way is to learn a handful of facts, and understand them. (*Anatomy of Riding*, 2004)

Great chefs do not need recipes because they understand the relationship between different ingredients, how they interact with each other, and what happens to them when they are cooked.

The problem with following any method – whether it is cooking or training horses – is that, unless we really understand the principles behind it, we are stuck with having to follow the method exactly. This reduces the number of options available to us when things do not go to plan. When it comes to training horses, even if we manage to memorize a whole host of instructions and somehow get them in the right order, there is no guarantee that the horse will co-operate. Horses are not machines, but individuals – living creatures with their own thoughts, emotions and priorities. And although horses are co-operative by nature,

the demands we make on them are so many and so varied that problems will inevitably arise – as anyone who has ever trained and/or ridden horses is only too well aware.

Right: *Sylvia Loch with her Lusitano x Thoroughbred gelding Espada.*

Below: *Classically trained horses often show great enthusiasm for their work. Sylvia Loch's Lusitano x TB gelding Espada loves showing off his Spanish Walk.*

If, on the other hand, we learn about the principles first, and take the trouble to understand them, we can build the necessary flexibility into our training and avoid the pitfalls of the 'one-size-fits-all' mentality.

Fortunately we do not need to reinvent the wheel. We already have a set of principles in place, worked out over centuries by great horsemen who took the trouble to study how horses move and use their bodies, and who formulated exercises that will strengthen the horse, make him supple and enable him to carry a rider with the minimum strain and risk of injury. These horsemen also discovered how riders can use their bodies to elicit responses from the horse; this is how we come to have the aids described in chapter 4. These principles, which are based on a sound understanding of equine physiology, are often referred to as 'classical', not only because some of the earliest such principles were established in classical Greece almost 2,400 years ago, but also because they embody harmony, balance, regularity and purity of form.

Many people believe that classical riding and training are somehow beyond the reach of the everyday rider because they think in terms of the Spanish Riding School and the Lipizzaners, or the extravagant Baroque horses of Portugal and Spain. I used to be one of those people, until I met a remarkable teacher, trainer and writer called Sylvia Loch. Through the clarity and integrity of her teaching and writing, Sylvia helped me to understand why I was not getting the results I wanted from my horses, and why so much of what I had been taught seemed either ineffective or confusing. She taught me that anyone – even people with moderate ability such as myself – can learn to ride and train their horse according to classical principles. I quickly found that, once I began to understand those principles, instead of focusing on the end result I started to become absorbed in the *process* of schooling my horses. Although, like most riders, I had had dreams of success in competition, those dreams started to matter less and less as I realized that what *was* important was the improvement I saw, on almost a daily basis, in my horses' way of going, athletic ability and general responsiveness. The horses themselves seemed more willing and even appeared to look forward to their work.

It is in the hope that other riders will be able to kindle the same enthusiasm in their horses through correct riding and schooling that I have written this book. It is aimed at riders who have progressed beyond the novice stage and now want to improve their horses and their own riding skills. It is not intended as a complete guide to training a horse from novice to advanced level, but rather as an explanation of the principles – often neglected or glossed over – which underlie correct training and riding, together with exercises to help riders improve their horses' basic education under saddle. It will enable riders to:

- recognize the aims of schooling and discover the basic principles of correct training;
- gain an understanding of what factors affect the horse's ability to use himself properly and carry a rider without strain and risk of injury;
- understand the importance of the rider's position in the saddle and how it affects the horse;
- learn the 'language of the aids' and how this can be used to influence the horse to his advantage, instead of simply giving a series of commands that he has to learn by rote;
- realize the importance of using tack that not only fits, but is also appropriate to the purpose for which it is being used;
- apply the principles of training to allow them to improve the horse's relaxation, balance, strength and suppleness;
- recognize the possible causes of some common problems and understand how to deal with these.

It is tempting, with a book such as this, to proceed straight to the chapters which tell us what to do in order to achieve certain aims, without first reading those chapters which will give us the tools – in this case, information – that will enable us to understand those aims properly. I hope readers will resist this temptation, because the earlier chapters contain the facts that will give them the necessary understanding. Such understanding cannot be complete because – as all great horsemen and women know – if there is one thing we should learn from training and riding horses, it is that the learning process never ends. The more knowledge we have, however, the greater our range of options for preventing problems, and for dealing with them if they do arise.

The purposes of schooling

ORSES ARE amazing creatures. Not only are they willing, co-operative and very trainable, but they are also shaped in such a way that riding them is comparatively easy – much easier than, say, riding a cow would be. The space just behind a horse's withers and shoulders is so perfectly shaped to take a saddle that it is tempting to forget that saddles have developed to fit that place, not the other way round. Some riders find it difficult to accept that correct riding and schooling are essential, because they think that horses are fine the way they are: look at the way they move at liberty. But such riders fail to consider how much we restrict that glorious movement when we get on a horse's back.

Below: We tend to take the free movement of horses at liberty for granted.

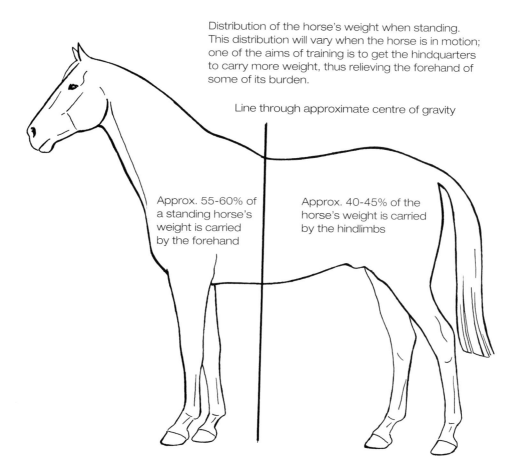

Distribution of the horse's weight when standing. This distribution will vary when the horse is in motion; one of the aims of training is to get the hindquarters to carry more weight, thus relieving the forehand of some of its burden.

Line through approximate centre of gravity

Approx. 55-60% of a standing horse's weight is carried by the forehand

Approx. 40-45% of the horse's weight is carried by the hindlimbs

Why horses need proper schooling

At liberty, a horse carries approximately 60 per cent of her weight on her forehand; this has been established by experiments involving force plates and weighbridges. The presence of a rider increases this amount considerably because the only place we can sit on a horse without either straining her back or getting tossed around to an unacceptable degree is just above the horse's centre of mass, which is closer to her forelegs than to her hind legs. So one of the aims of schooling is to strengthen the horse's hind legs so that they can relieve the more vulnerable forelegs of some of the strain. Proper schooling is essential if we are to train the horse to carry herself and her rider with the maximum efficiency and the minimum expenditure of effort, and reduce the potential for strain to her joints and muscles.

Many people dislike the idea of schooling and tend to regard it as boring and unproductive work consisting of endless trotting round in circles. That is not schooling; it is simply trotting round in circles!

Above: Distribution of weight on forehand and hind legs.

Below: Horses can move more freely when unencumbered by a rider. This mare tends to stiffen under a rider and becomes difficult to manoeuvre.

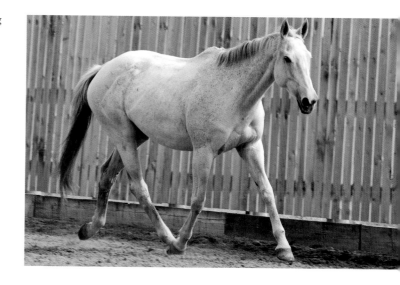

What does schooling entail?

Schooling consists of exercises to relax the horse, improve her balance, strengthen her muscles and increase her suppleness. These exercises include transitions, bends, circles and loops, voltes, quarter-turns and progressive lateral work. Some of them, such as the shoulder-in, form part of certain dressage tests, as do the school movements that are described in chapters 6–8. These should never, however, be thought of as simply movements that have to be learned in order to perform dressage tests. Even the most advanced movements, such as the *passage*, *piaffe* and the canter pirouette, were originally intended as training exercises – the equivalent of a university education for the horse. They were never meant to be taken out of context simply to be ridden in dressage competitions. Indeed, the masters of equitation who, between the seventeenth and eighteenth centuries devised so many of the training exercises we use today, would not understand our current pigeonholing of such exercises into something called 'dressage'. For them, a 'dressed' horse was simply a horse who had been fully trained for riding.

The classical training principles

The exercises described in this book were developed and enhanced over the course of many centuries by the masters of classical horsemanship referred to in the introduction. They are all based on the principles of training which take into account the horse's anatomy, physiology and psychology, and therefore do not seek to impose on her something which is alien to her. You might think that there is nothing natural about asking horses to trot in circles, move sideways or perform high school movements such as the *passage* and *piaffe* referred to earlier. If we watch horses at liberty, however, we can see that in fact they do all of these things, whether in play, in display (for example, a stallion showing off to mares or intimidating rivals) or simply in the process of getting from one place to another. Our task is to use these natural movements in ways which will enhance the horse's natural athletic ability under saddle.

Above: The school movements have their origins in natural equine behaviour, especially in display behaviour. This Morgan stallion could be performing a natural – albeit less polished – version of the High School passage.

The German scales of training

We can understand and apply the principles of training much more effectively if we organize them into some kind of system. In the realms of dressage, the German 'scales of training' are taught all over the world. They set out the principles underlying every aspect of correct training under saddle, and we should not think of them as concerning only dressage riders. They – or at least the principles they embody – should be understood by every rider who wants to improve their horse, even if all they intend to do is have fun. Not all classical trainers follow the scales of training exactly as they are set out here; in Portugal and Spain, in particular, the character of the Iberian horses often needs a rather different emphasis (see chapter 9 for more about this).

Even so, all classical trainers use the principles embodied in the scales of training, which are given below, together with the chapter(s) in which they are discussed in this book.

Relaxation

Before we can achieve anything meaningful with the horse, she must be free of tension, which will lock up her muscles and her mind, and prevent her from using her body correctly. (Chapters 2 and 6.)

Rhythm

The regularity of the paces should be maintained regardless of whether the horse is working on straight lines or in circles, turns or transitions. (Chapters 2, 4, 6, 7 and 8.)

Above: Maintain the regularity of the paces regardless of whether the horse is working on straight lines, in circles, turns or transitions.

Left: Before we can achieve anything meaningful with horses, they must be free from tension. This horse's soft eyes and general demeanour show that he is quite relaxed. When this photograph was taken he was being re-educated to accept a bit.

Contact

This forms the connection between the rider's hand and the horse's mouth. As the muscles of the horse's neck, back and hindquarters form a continuous 'chain', the connection goes all the way down to the horse's hind feet. The rider does not make the contact by setting the horse's head; instead the horse makes the contact by seeking the bit. (Chapters 2, 3, 4, 5 and 6.)

Above: Impulsion has nothing to do with speed; it is produced when the energy created by the hind legs is transformed into forward movement.

Below: Suppling exercises will help to straighten horses once they are moving rhythmically and in balance.

Above: The rider does not make the contact by setting the horse's head; instead the horse makes the contact by seeking the bit.

Impulsion

Impulsion has nothing to do with speed; it is produced when the energy created by the hind legs is transformed into forward movement. Green horses often run on when ridden because they lose their balance; correct training will help them to find their balance and enable them to move freely with power and rhythm. (Chapters 2, 6, 7 and 8.)

Straightness

Like humans, most horses are born with a bias towards one side or the other – what we call left- or right-handedness. This means that they will tend to be slightly crooked in movement. When ridden, they need to distribute their weight evenly on both sides of the body; otherwise one side will become strained as a result of carrying more of the

rider's weight. Suppling exercises will help to straighten the horse once she is moving rhythmically and in balance. (Chapters 3, 4, 6, 7 and 8.)

Collection

Horses usually carry more than half their weight on their forelegs. The aim of gymnastic training is to relieve some of this weight – which is increased by that of the rider – and transfer some of the load from the forelegs to the hind legs. The horse is thus enabled to move in balance and self-carriage throughout all the gaits, ready at any moment to move forwards, sideways or even backwards, with minimal effort. She is then said to be *collected*.

The scales of training are usually laid out in the order in which they are shown on pages 15–16, but we should not think of this as a set order which has to be followed rigidly. With some horses you might find that impulsion has to come before relaxation, or that contact comes before rhythm, and so on. So much depends on the individual horse, her physical type, psychology, and how she has previously been trained. We must always devise a training approach to suit the horse; there should never be any question of simply following a training 'recipe'. Fortunately, the great thing about these principles is that once we understand them we can use them to create training strategies which are flexible enough to suit any horse.

Where to school

Most schooling exercises are carried out under saddle, but they may also include work from the ground, whether in hand or on the lunge. Schooling does not necessarily have to be carried out in a proper arena; a corner of a field will do, as long as it is reasonably flat. Some exercises can also be performed while you are out on a hack or trail ride with your horse. Make use of natural features such as hedges, telegraph poles, rocks, trees and bushes to act as markers for finding a straight line and making transitions. Use hills and steep inclines to encourage the horse to engage her hindquarters, as described in chapter 8. Many people are never in a position to school their horse in an arena, yet with a little ingenuity they are still able to produce horses who are schooled and supple to a high degree.

If you are having to use part of a large field, you will need to find some way of partitioning off that section from the rest of the field. Wide open spaces are an invitation to horses to become overexuberant, and you will find it very difficult to get a horse to concentrate if she is thinking of having a fling in the field. If fencing off part of the field is not an option, it might be possible to use old straw or hay bales as a perimeter.

Regardless of whether you do your schooling in a purpose-built arena, a corner of a field or out on a hack or trail ride, think about the kind of surface you are riding on and how it affects your horse's joints, tendons, ligaments and muscles. A too-hard surface will cause injuries to joints from concussion, whereas a surface that is too soft may provide insufficient traction and, especially if it is deep, may create strain injuries to the muscles, tendons and ligaments of the limbs and back. Some of the best places to ride can be old, well-maintained parklands where the grass is kept short and the soil is well drained, resulting in a springy surface which allows horses to move freely without fear of strain or concussion. If you are able to ride in such a setting, you are very fortunate indeed. Most of us, however, have to make do with what is available in the area where we

Left: Horses normally carry more than half their weight on their forelegs. The aim of gymnastic training is to relieve some of this weight – which is increased by that of the rider – and transfer some of the load from the forelegs to the hind legs.

live, and the nature of riding terrain depends largely on the local climate and environment.

Marking out the schooling area

Many of the most effective schooling exercises are incorporated into arena patterns which help riders to structure schooling sessions so as to maximize the effectiveness of the exercises. You will find it easier to ride these patterns if you mark out your schooling area. A standard dressage arena measures 40 m (131 ft) by

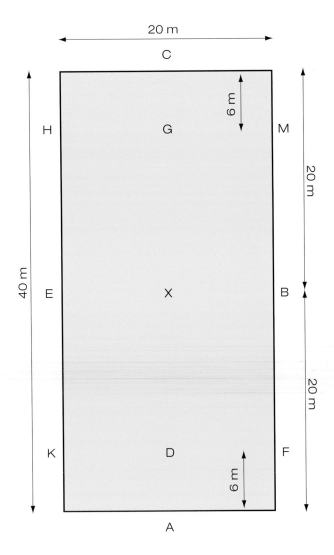

Above: A standard arena.

Above right: A competition arena.

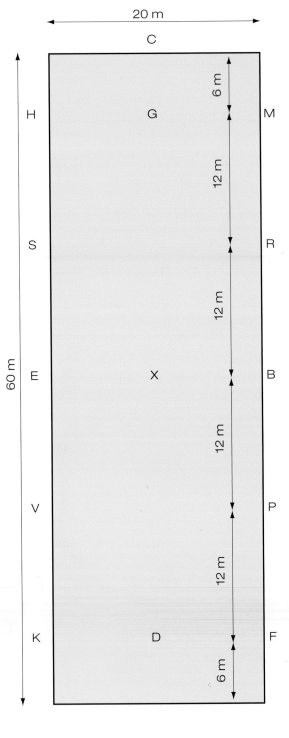

20 m (66 ft), while a competition arena measures 60 m (197 ft). Even if you do not have access to a purpose-built arena, you should try to make your schooling area as large as you can and, if possible, as near to the dimensions of the standard arena as you can get (see above left). Ponies and small- to medium-sized horses (up to 160 cm/15.3hh) can

Above: A purpose-built arena is an advantage, but it is not essential.

Right: You should try to make your schooling area as large as you can and as near to the dimensions of the standard arena as possible.

Below right: Proper dressage markers may be obtained from tack shops and mail-order outlets.

make do with less than the standard area. Larger horses (162.5 cm (16 hh) and over), however, really need 40 m by 20 m or more, as otherwise they may find it difficult to maintain a canter in what is, for them, a relatively small space.

Markers in the form of letters are positioned at set intervals to enable riders to ride the school figures accurately (see the illustrations on the left for the measurements and positioning of these letters). You can buy proper dressage markers from tack shops and mail-order outlets; however, if you do not want to go to this expense, small traffic cones make excellent markers to which letters can be attached easily. Cones such as that shown in the photograph on page 20 can be purchased from retailers specializing in equipment for sporting events. I have suggested traffic cones because they are lightweight, easy to move, readily visible and will not cause injuries if a horse catches one with her foot, but you can use anything you like provided it does not create a hazard for either horse or rider.

Above: Traffic cones make excellent markers because they are lightweight, easy to move, readily visible and will not cause injuries if a horse catches one with a foot.

Right: Small traffic cones like this one can be purchased from retailers specializing in equipment for sporting events.

Below: If you have to share a schooling area, certain conventions have to be observed for safety's sake. These riders have agreed to ride side by side but in general riders need to keep away from each other when schooling.

Arena etiquette

If you are lucky enough to have the use of a purpose-built arena, you may have to share it with other riders. Observance of arena etiquette is not an outdated formality, but a form of consideration for other riders and their horses, which is essential if annoyance, frustration and potentially dangerous accidents are to be avoided.

Once we realize the benefits it can bring to our horses, we can see that correct schooling is a worthwhile and necessary pursuit. If we make the schooling sessions as interesting and as varied as possible, the horse will begin to find it worthwhile, too. As classical trainer Erik F. Herbermann has observed:

> Contrary to popular belief, horses do not get bored with basic work. If the rider demands exact responses, paying close attention to detail and quality, neither horse nor rider will have time to get bored; rather, a true sense of accomplishment will be gained.
> (*Dressage Formula*, 1999)

The general rules are:

- When entering the school, make sure you do not disturb other riders already working. You should agree with other users beforehand what warning will be given before a rider enters an occupied school.
- If mounting in the school itself, lead your horse to the centre of the school and position her parallel to the short side, so that you can mount without disturbing other riders.
- Right of way is normally given to riders on the left rein (although this may vary in some countries, so make sure that you all agree beforehand about which rein is given priority). So if you are riding on the track on the right rein and a rider comes towards you on the left rein, you should bring your horse in off the track and continue parallel to it until you come to the next corner, when you can return to the track (unless another rider is approaching on the left rein!).
- When riding in walk, keep well away from the track so that those riding in trot or canter have sufficient room to pass each other in safety.
- Passing another rider should be carried out only as described above, not by overtaking, which could cause an accident. If coming up fast behind another rider, turn away and either ride a circle until the other rider is safely out of the way, or turn across the school to the other long side.
- When riding the school exercises described in chapters 6–8, always leave sufficient room for other riders. If necessary, come to a mutual agreement about who will be practising in which areas of the school.

Top left: *Riders should observe arena etiquette when passing each other in the schooling area.*

Above: *Correct schooling is a worthwhile and necessary pursuit. Here a pupil is having a formal lesson with renowned teacher Sylvia Loch.*

Equine physiology and physical responses

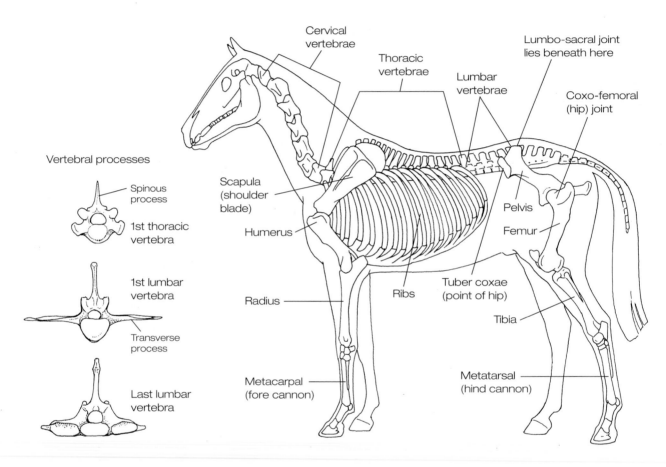

Cervical vertebrae

Thoracic vertebrae

Lumbar vertebrae

Lumbo-sacral joint lies beneath here

Coxo-femoral (hip) joint

Vertebral processes

Spinous process

1st thoracic vertebra

1st lumbar vertebra

Transverse process

Last lumbar vertebra

Scapula (shoulder blade)

Humerus

Radius

Metacarpal (fore cannon)

Ribs

Tuber coxae (point of hip)

Pelvis

Femur

Tibia

Metatarsal (hind cannon)

BEFORE WE can train a horse in a way that will enhance his natural athletic ability and enable him to carry a rider without damaging his musculo-skeletal system, we need to understand how that system works. As the horse's skeleton cannot move or even stand up on its own, we will concern ourselves mainly with the muscles and connective tissues such as ligaments and tendons. These hold the skeleton together and enable horses to move in the fluid, graceful manner that makes them so enchanting to watch.

***Above:** Horse skeleton.*

Voluntary muscles

The muscles in question are the so-called 'voluntary' muscles, which as the name suggests are under the horse's voluntary control, unlike those of the digestive, circulatory and reproductive systems, the actions of which are all involuntary. The term voluntary in this context is slightly misleading because, although the horse *can* move such muscles voluntarily, there are certain stimuli that produce a reaction that is virtually automatic. This reaction is known as a reflex and, as we shall see, reflex actions play a vital part in the horse–rider interaction. There are more than 700 so-called voluntary muscles in the horse's body, but we are concerned mainly with some of the muscle groups that maintain posture, support the back and create movement in the ridden horse.

The muscles responsible for movement are able to contract and relax rapidly because they are composed of bundles of long fibres. They are unable to maintain tension for a prolonged period of time, and if forced to do so will accumulate lactic acid, which leads to cramps and their resulting severe pain. The shorter muscles which serve to maintain posture are more able to sustain tension without damage because they contract and relax more slowly than the longer muscles which enable movement.

Connective tissues

Muscles are attached to bones by the fibrous, inelastic connective tissues called tendons; when a muscle contracts – for example, to flex a joint – it is the tendons which transmit the force of the contraction to the relevant bones. Ligaments are more elastic than tendons; one of their main jobs is to hold the bones of movable joints together and prevent them from moving too much, to avoid dislocation of the joint.

As well as being attached to bones, muscles may be attached to the sheets of dense fibrous connective tissue known as 'fascia'. The fascia may enclose a muscle in a way that separates it from neighbouring muscles and enables it to function independently. Alternatively, it may bind groups of muscles together so that, although they each have their own function, they do not act in isolation from the muscles to which they are bound.

Through the medium of this connective tissue, the muscles of the hindlimbs are connected to those of the forelimbs via the back muscles, forming what is often referred to as a 'chain' of muscles. In the same way, the muscles of the topline are linked to those of the bottom line of the horse's torso. As the rest of this chapter will show, this has far-reaching implications for the ridden horse.

Below: The main ligaments of the neck, back and hindquarters.

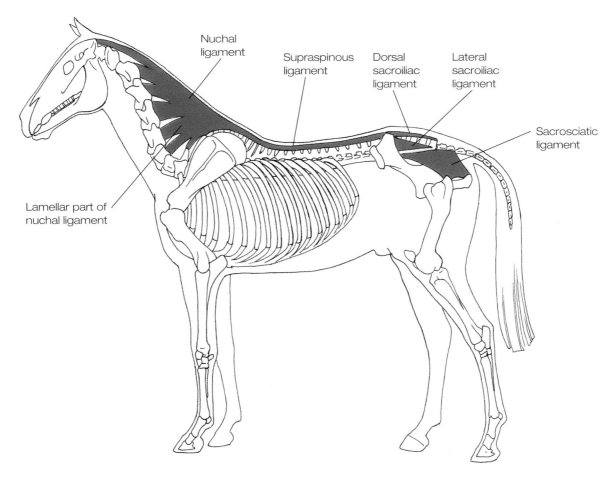

Nuchal ligament

Supraspinous ligament

Dorsal sacroiliac ligament

Lateral sacroiliac ligament

Sacrosciatic ligament

Lamellar part of nuchal ligament

The horse's back

The main function of the horse's back muscles is to transmit movement from the hindquarters to the forehand. In addition, various muscles and ligaments form a kind of sling which, together with the mass of connective tissue which extends the length of the underside of the horse's belly (the so-called linea alba, or 'white line'), acts as a support for the heavy internal organs.

For the horse, freedom of movement depends on the freedom of his back muscles to contract and lengthen. As the muscles which move the hindlimbs contract to flex the coxo-femoral (hip) and lumbo-sacral joints to bring the hind leg forwards, the gluteal (gluteus medius) muscle on that side has to lengthen in order to allow the hind leg to come forwards. As the gluteus medius is attached to the longissimus muscle of the back, that, too, must lengthen. When the hind foot lands on the ground, the hind leg supports the horse's body weight (known as the 'stance phase'), then the joints of the hindlimb flex, the hoof pushes against the ground and the hindlimb extends to propel the horse forwards. The gluteus medius (and therefore, the longissimus) has to contract again in order to allow the coxo-femoral joint to extend and the hindlimb to straighten. At the walk and trot, the lengthening and contraction of the longissimus occurs on each side of the spine alternately; in the canter and gallop, they occur simultaneously on each side.

The addition of a rider's weight will tend to stiffen the long back muscles and prevent them from lengthening and contracting sufficiently for the hindlimbs to move freely and efficiently. Freedom of movement of the horse's shoulders and forelimbs is also affected. This is because the longissimus is covered by another important back muscle, the latissimus, which inserts onto the humerus, one of the principal bones involved in movement of the forehand. So what enables the horse to carry a rider without locking up his back muscles?

Below: Chain (or 'ring') of muscles.

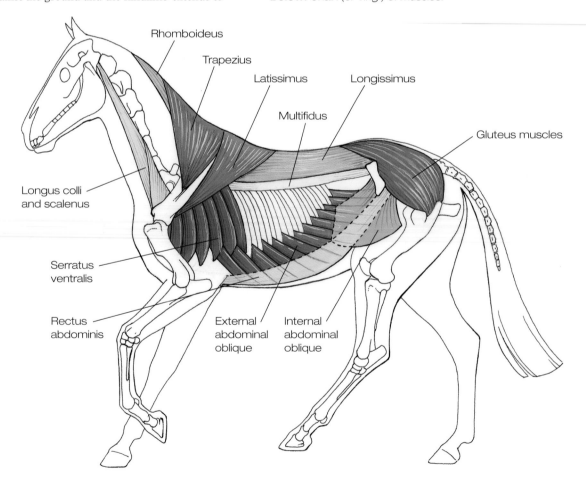

Left: When the hind foot lands on the ground, the hind leg supports the horse's body weight.

Below left: The hind limb flexes, then the hoof pushes against the ground and the hind limb extends again to propel the horse forward.

Below: The abdominal muscles assist with bracing the back; this can be seen at its most extreme when a horse urinates or defecates.

Bracing the horse's back

If we look at the horse's spine (see illustration, page 22), we can see that the thoracic vertebrae have both vertical (spinous) and horizontal (transverse) projections (known as 'processes'). These vary in height, width and direction depending on their position along the spine. The vertical processes are linked at the tips by two powerful ligaments. These are the nuchal ligament, which runs from the rear of the skull to the third thoracic vertebra, and its extension, the supraspinous ligament, which continues beyond the third thoracic vertebra as far as the sacrum.

A dense sheet of ligamentous fibre called the lamella attaches the nuchal ligament to the vertebrae of the neck (cervical vertebrae). Adjacent to the lamella, on both sides, are muscles which support the head and neck.

As we saw earlier, ligaments have a certain amount of elasticity. If the horse stretches his neck forwards, the nuchal ligament stretches, too. It pulls on the spinous processes at the withers, which act like a lever, producing tension on the supraspinous ligament and the deep muscles of the back which lie on either side of the spine. This tension acts to stabilize the spine and allows the back muscles concerned with locomotion to get on with their job. The abdominal muscles, mainly the rectus abdominis and the external oblique muscles, assist the nuchal ligament and the deep back muscles in this; traction on these muscles reinforces traction along the topline. Try bracing your abdominal muscles and you will feel the corresponding bracing of the muscles of your lower back. This is why people with lower back pain are usually given exercises to strengthen the abdominal muscles which support the back.

If the rider tries to raise the horse's head and neck (whether by pulling on the reins or raising the hands)

before the longus colli and scaleni muscles at the base of the neck are strong enough, the horse will tense the rhomboideus and trapezius muscles. The rhomboideus lies on either side of the crest of the neck, while the trapezius partly overlies the rhomboideus and attaches to the shoulder blade. This tension will make the base of the neck sink, and traction on the nuchal and supraspinous ligaments will be lost. As the spine no longer has the support of these ligaments, the withers – which are not attached to the shoulder blades – will sink down between the shoulders, the horse's back will hollow and, because the long back muscles then have to take over the role of supporting the rider's weight, the hindquarters will be unable to engage and the hocks will trail because the horse cannot flex the joints of his hind legs properly. This robs them of much of their propulsive power as well as their shock-absorbing qualities. Observers are sometimes fooled by

Above: If we look only at the head and neck, this looks like a good outline; however, the horse's back and withers are not raised, and he is not truly engaging his hindquarters. However, unlike many horses nowadays, he is not being forced into a false head carriage.

horses who flex the hocks and lift the hind feet quite high, moving them forwards in a kind of 'bicycling' action which generates a lot of up-and-down movement of the croup, but not much forward movement (and certainly not much impulsion!). This can look quite impressive, but is in fact all show and no 'go'; it is wasteful of effort and potentially damaging to the horse's forehand, as it does nothing to protect the limbs from concussion.

On the other hand, if the horse is allowed to stretch his head and neck out, eventually his neck muscles will strengthen because they have to support the weight of his head. They will fill out at the base and along their topline, and the longus colli and scaleni will be able to raise the vertebrae at the junction of the neck with the thorax, making it seem as if the horse has grown at the withers. Eventually, as the horse engages his hindquarters more and takes more weight on his hindlimbs, the quarters will lower and the whole forehand will appear to lift; this is what we see when the horse is in true collection.

This is why it is so important that the ridden horse works in a good outline: not because it will impress dressage judges or because it looks good, but because it is the only way a horse can carry a rider without strain. The outline made by an untrained or novice horse will be longer and lower than that of a more advanced horse, but with correct training and riding all horses, except those who have serious conformation problems, will be able to work in

Below: *A horse working in a correct outline will raise his neck and withers naturally.*

the more rounded outline which marks the beginning of collection. I must emphasize, though, that it is the horse who makes the outline, not the rider; any attempt to pull the horse into a false outline (that is, with the head and neck tucked in, which is what many people imagine a good outline to be), will have the effect described previously, of disconnecting the chain of muscles which enables the horse to work correctly. All the rider does is receive the power generated by the hindquarters in the hand, which is mostly passive (as chapters 3 and 4 will show).

Fortunately there are certain aspects of the horse's anatomy which will help the rider in his or her task of

Below: *When a horse who is being led in hand refuses to move forward, we can usually get him to move by turning his head and neck to one side; his proprioceptive sense makes him want to regain his balance.*

getting the horse to work in a way that will protect his back and forelimbs while encouraging him to flex the joints of his hindlimbs.

Proprioception

The muscles, ligaments and tendons contain specialized cells called 'proprioceptors' which inform the central nervous system, via the sensory nerves, about stimuli affecting the maintenance of balance and muscle co-ordination. Proprioception is the nervous system's way of keeping track of the body's movements and the position of its various parts at any one time. It is an unconscious process, often referred to as a kind of sixth sense: animals (including, of course, humans) are aware of where their bodies and limbs are and what they are doing without having to think about it. It is this proprioceptive sense which enables horses to clear obstacles with their hind feet;

they automatically know where their hind feet are in relation to the rest of their bodies. Some horses are better at this than others. In the same way that some foals develop their proprioceptive sense – which enables them to stand and run about soon after birth – more quickly than others, some horses have to learn to judge when to take off over a jump in order to lift their hind feet at the right time. Once they have learned this, however, it becomes an automatic response – just like motor skills learned by humans, such as the co-ordination necessary for driving a car.

The stimuli to which the proprioceptive cells respond may consist of pressure, movement or stretching. Trainers often talk about turning a horse in terms of positioning his head: point the head in the right direction, they say, and the rest of the body will follow. This is perfectly correct. The displacement of the head causes the proprioceptive cells to send signals to the nervous system, informing it that the body's balance is being affected. Further nerve impulses are then relayed to the appropriate body parts, telling them to correct the horse's balance by moving the rest of the body in the direction of the perceived imbalance. This is why, when a horse who is being led in hand refuses to move forwards, we can usually get him to move by turning his head and neck to one side. His proprioceptive sense tells his nervous system that his balance is being affected, and his reflex response makes him respond accordingly.

The intercostal nerves

The horse's trunk is richly supplied with a system of nerves that issue directly from the spinal cord itself. These nerves divide into upper and lower branches; the lower branches subdivide again, and it is those branches which pass between the intercostal muscles (that is, the muscles which lie between the ribs) that interest us here.

It is these intercostal nerves that enable the rider to 'talk' to the horse through the medium of touch. They lie very close to the surface, and each time the rider's legs touch the horse's sides this stimulates the underlying nerves which affect the horse's back muscles. We can easily test this by pressing lightly against the horse's side, which will make the horse retract his side away from the pressure. As chapter 6 will show, many classical trainers use this reflex response when working horses in hand. If both the rider's legs stimulate the horse's sides, the effect is to raise the part of the back that lies directly above the nerves being

Above: If the leg is used on one side only, this will create lateral flexion – hence the term 'bending the horse round the rider's leg'.

stimulated. If the leg is used on one side only, this will create lateral flexion – hence the term 'bending the horse around the rider's leg'.

As Sara Wyche observes:

> This movement, this lifting of the chest cavity in response to pressure from the rider's legs, is the most fundamental ingredient of riding. It is the key to everything that follows, both in terms of the horse's anatomy and in terms of the sequential application of the rider's aids. This, and nothing else, is the passport to impulsion, the gateway to lightness. Understanding the importance of the rider's legs is to have, at once, discovered the Theory of Everything. (*The Anatomy of Riding*, 2004)

The intercostal nerves perform yet another function vital to the ridden horse. The powerful rectus abdominis muscle runs from the fourth rib all the way up to the pubis, which lies just in front of the coxo-femoral joint; it also

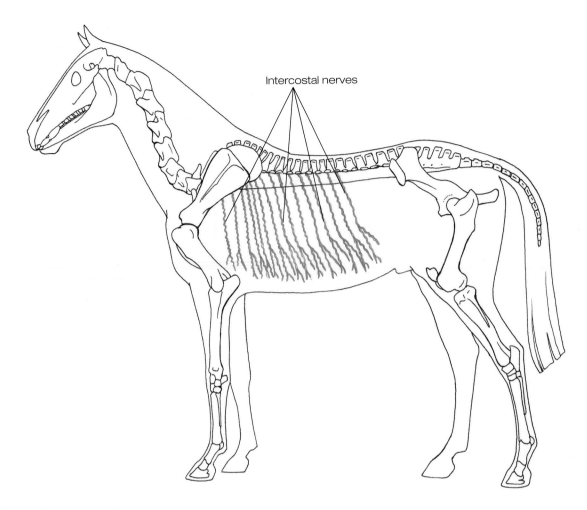

Intercostal nerves

Above: *The intercostal nerves.*

connects to the linea alba. In this way it has several roles: it helps to support the organs of the abdomen; when stimulated on one side it contributes to lateral bending on that side; and, because of its point of insertion on the pelvis, stimulation of the nerves which affect the rectus abdominis makes it contract, which flexes the lumbo-sacral joint, assisting engagement of the hindquarters. The external oblique abdominal muscle originates on the ribs and terminates on the fascia above the stifle. Stimulation of the intercostal nerves on one side will cause this muscle to contract and flex the coxo-femoral joint, bringing the hindlimb forwards (see above).

Although these responses created by stimulation of the intercostal nerves are reflex responses, they are not totally automatic. If the horse is tense, his muscles may be unable to respond in this way, or the way in which the leg aids are given may actively prevent him from responding. Riders are often told to squeeze the horse's sides with their legs. This presumably came about as an antidote to the idea of kicking in order to get the horse to move. While kicking is certainly unpleasant for the horse, squeezing can be equally so, as well as being ineffective. The horse's lungs lie almost directly below the area where the rider's legs act, so any constriction in this area is bound to affect his breathing.

There is another, very good reason why squeezing is counter-productive. I imagine most of us have, at some time or another, sat for some time in a position which results in numbness in one or both legs. This numbness comes about because of continuous pressure on the leg nerves. This pressure blocks the electrical impulses which pass along the nerve fibres to the brain and spinal cord; when the pressure is eased, the nerve impulses can continue on their way, and the numbness is replaced by the tingling, prickling sensation often referred to as 'pins and needles'.

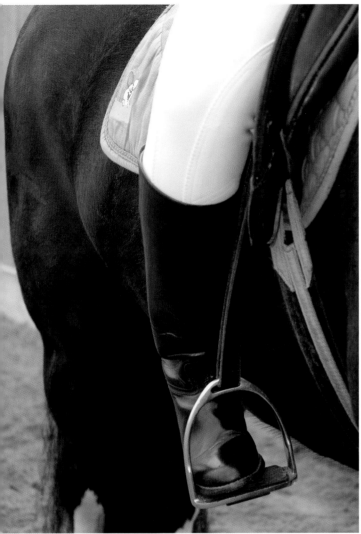

Now if we think of all the nerves which lie very close to the surface along the horse's ribcage, and which we make use of when riding him, we can see that any prolonged squeezing in this area may not only (literally) take his breath away, but also actually prevent him from complying with our requests to move forwards. As Sara Wyche remarks:

> The time span between [nerve] impulses is very short, measured only in seconds. Nevertheless, the difference between legs that 'massage' the horse's sides, and legs that try to squeeze the life out of them, is the difference between a horse that can produce an elastic stride and one that produces nothing at all. (*The Anatomy of Riding*, 2004)

Above left: *Riders are often told to squeeze the horse's sides with their legs, but this is counter-productive.*

Top right: *We use the leg at or just behind the girth because we want the horse's back to be raised underneath the rider's seat. This helps to counteract the effects of the rider's weight and aids the horse in raising his forehand.*

Above: *If the leg is used too far behind the girth the horse's back will be raised nearer the loin. This will tend to tip the horse onto his forehand.*

Above: Using the leg too far forward will affect the forehand but it will do nothing to raise the back or stimulate flexion of the hindlimbs.

So we need to think in terms of giving brief, light, positive touches with the leg rather than squeezing or thumping – both of which will be at best ineffective and at worst counter-productive.

It is important to remember that *where* we give the leg aids is also important. The reason why we use the leg at or just behind the girth is that we want the horse's back to be raised underneath the rider's seat, as this helps to counteract the effects of the rider's weight and aids the horse in raising his forehand. If the leg is used too far behind the girth (for example, by riders kicking up and backwards, which often happens), the horse's back will be raised nearer the loin. This tends to tip the horse onto his forehand and as a result blocks impulsion from the hindquarters. Using the leg too far forwards will affect the forehand; stimulation of the nerves affecting the serratus ventralis muscle just behind the horse's elbow will help to produce a forward-reaching stride, but it will do nothing to raise the back or stimulate flexion of the hindlimbs. As long as we understand this, we can use the leg in different places in order to produce specific results (for more on this, see page 63).

Above: If we could view this horse from above we would see that there is a bend in his spine.

Is bend in the horse's back an illusion?

According to some trainers, bend in the horse's back *is* an illusion. They believe that, as the horse's spine is relatively rigid (except at the neck, where a considerable amount of bend is possible), the concept of bending throughout its length (required for work on a circle to be of any benefit) is more one of imagery than a reflection of reality.

Experiments carried out on equine cadavers and on living horses have shown, however, that horses' spines do indeed bend. Certainly, the amount of this bend is limited by the ribcage, the connective tissues and the transverse processes of the spine. Nevertheless, a small amount of movement of each vertebral joint translates into quite a lot of bend when measured along the length of the thoracic spine. The greatest amount of bend occurs between the fourth and eighteenth (or nineteenth) thoracic vertebrae; the least amount occurs along the lumbar spine because of the length of the transverse processes here. So, yes, horses can certainly bend – enough to create a fairly even bend from nose to tail.

The chain of muscles

Earlier in this chapter I referred to the co-called 'chain of muscles'. It is literally true that what goes on in the horse's mouth affects what happens in his hind feet. The muscles of the jaw and those attached to the base of the tongue are connected to the muscles of the neck, shoulders and thorax. Discomfort in the mouth results in unwanted tension in the muscles of the neck, shoulders and back, and, as we have seen, what happens in the back affects the hindlimbs also. If we put undue pressure on the bit, causing tension in the jaw, we can effectively 'lock up' the whole system from mouth to hind legs. This is why misguided attempts to put a horse 'on the bit' by fixing the hand and driving the horse into a strong contact can have such a detrimental effect on the horse's ability to move properly.

The detrimental effects of overbending

For the horse to be able to lift his neck at the withers and maintain an even traction along the nuchal and supraspinous ligaments, he must be able to reach forwards to seek a contact with the bit. Unfortunately, it is now very common for horses to be ridden with their necks overbent, sometimes so much so that their heads are almost touching their chests. Sadly for the horse, this overbent posture is insufficiently penalized in the dressage arena. All too many riders, seeing this posture rewarded by high marks, think that it must be correct. Nothing could be further from the

Below: The so-called 'chain of muscles' (sometimes referred to as the 'ring of muscles') links the horse's mouth with his hind feet, and his top line with his bottom line. This young colt is stretching his topline; his abdominal muscles assist with this.

Above: *Overbending: this horse is only slightly overbent but his neck is shortened and his stride length will be restricted as a result.*

Left: *The horse must be able to reach forward to seek a contact with the bit.*

truth. Horses may sometimes overbend, especially if they are tired, but this is easily corrected by the rider sending them on more vigorously (then, hopefully, allowing the horse to have a rest). Don't be tempted to follow the trend towards overbending, however – if the horse is consistently worked in an overbent posture for any length of time he will suffer because:

• the nuchal ligament is overtightened at the poll, which may result in injury to the ligament;
• the horse cannot lift the base of his neck because the ligament is overtight at the poll and slackened at the withers;
• the position of his head squashes his windpipe, meaning that he cannot breathe properly;
• tension at the poll affects the muscles of the face and jaw, preventing the horse from relaxing his jaw to accept the bit comfortably;
• uneven stretching of the nuchal ligament reduces traction to its continuation, the supraspinous ligament, forcing the long back muscles to take over the role of supporting the spine;
• as a result of the above, the back muscles become stiff and tense, and the horse is unable to engage his hindlimbs properly.

The rider's interaction with the horse

THIS CHAPTER deals with how the rider interacts with the horse and the ways in which the rider affects the horse's athletic abilities.

The importance of sitting correctly

We have only to think of carrying a badly packed rucksack or giving a squirming child a piggy-back (pick-a-back) ride to understand how difficult it must be for the horse to carry a rider who shifts about in the saddle and does not sit in balance. Only recently I spent an afternoon carrying a camera with a long, heavy lens, in a waist-belt pack. After walking for only ten minutes or so with the camera positioned over my left hip, I began to feel excruciating pain in my right hip joint and lower back. I was able to stop to redistribute the weight more comfortably; the horse can

Below: *A dressage rider.* **Opposite:** *Saddle seat rider.*

make her discomfort known only through resistances, which often result in her being blamed for being disobedient or unruly!

Many riders may be unconvinced by the idea that what the rider does in the saddle is so important because there are so many different ways of riding horses, depending on the discipline in question. There is the dressage seat, hunter seat, saddle seat, stock seat, western seat etc., as well as the different positions adopted by jockeys, showjumpers and eventers. All of these ways of riding are adapted to the discipline in question, so how can we talk about a 'correct' seat?

Perhaps we should forget about specific disciplines and consider just *how* the way a rider sits on a horse affects the horse and her ability to respond correctly. As Dr Deb Bennett says:

All domestic horses belong to one species and have one skeletal design operated by one set of physiological reflexes. Therefore, there are really only two ways to ride – with the horse or against him. ('True Collection', *Equus*, 1994)

Above: *A showjumping rider.*

So regardless of our chosen discipline (or even if we choose to ride simply for pleasure), if we want to enhance our horse's performance and make it easy for her to carry a rider, we have to think about how our presence in the saddle affects her. We have to sit in such a way that we can relieve her burden and restore her freedom of movement under saddle. This means that we should not think in terms of a different seat for each discipline, but rather about a neutral 'classical' seat from which we can adapt our position and movements according to what is required at any specific time.

As we saw in chapter 2, the weight of a rider on a horse's back affects her ability to move freely because of the tendency to stiffen her back under the weight. Brigadier

General Kurt Albrecht, former Director of the Spanish Riding School, points out that: 'An incorrect posture of the rider is the root cause of innumerable difficulties in controlling direction and also of faulty carriage of the horse.' The rider must therefore sit in such a way that the horse's back muscles are free to carry out their function of supporting the spine and transmitting the movement of the hind legs to the forehand. This means that riders must take responsibility for their weight by sitting in balance over their base of support (the feet) and with sufficient muscle tone to remain relatively still (that is, without making any involuntary movements that will upset the horse's balance or send her unintentional signals).

Unfortunately, riders have a tendency *not* to take responsibility for their weight; instead, they hand that over to the horse, who may then be left to struggle on her own to remain in balance under this unbalanced weight. So much of what we do on horseback is affected by the way we think about it. The idea of sitting on a horse encourages us to think in terms of sitting on a chair, which does not help us to assume the correct posture in the saddle. And, as chapter 5 will show, the design of many saddles means that riders have little option but to adopt what is often called the 'chair' seat: in other words, they sit as if they were on a chair, with their feet out in front of them. One test of a balanced seat is to imagine what would happen to a rider if the horse were magically removed from underneath them. Would the rider remain in balance, or would they topple over? If we look at all too many riders, we can see that they would simply topple over backwards. Look at the photograph on page 40. What do you think would happen to this rider in such a scenario?

Below: The horse must be able to raise his back under the rider's weight. This Arabian stallion is certainly demonstrating this in a rather exuberant canter.

The 'chair' seat and the 'crotch' seat

The chair seat is not only unbalanced, but also makes it very difficult for riders to use their legs in a position where they can be effective. In addition, it means the rider's weight is concentrated on a very small area of the horse's back – which, as we shall see, is bad news for the horse.

On the other hand, if we look at the photograph on page 41, we can see that this rider has problems of a different nature. Whereas the rider in the first photograph would topple over backwards, this rider might well fall flat on his face, although he could possibly regain his balance by taking a little jump forwards. By tipping forwards and sitting too much on his crotch and inner thighs, he is

Below: A chair seat. If the horse were to be removed from under the rider, the latter would simply topple over backwards.

overweighting the horse's forehand even further. He is looking down, which adds to his lack of balance, as we shall see later in this chapter. Both riders are making life difficult – not only for the horse, but also for themselves.

The classical seat

A simple exercise carried out while standing up will help us to understand how the classical position should feel and why it works in practice.

Exercise 1

1. Stand up straight, in an upright but relaxed posture, with

Above: If the horse were to be removed, this rider might well fall flat on his face, although he could possibly save himself by taking a little jump forwards to regain his balance.

your feet as far apart as they would be if you were sitting on a horse, with your arms hanging loosely by your sides.

2. Shrug your shoulders, lifting them high enough to have the sensation that they are almost touching the tips of your ear lobes. Then move your shoulders back and down again; this will flatten your shoulder blades and you should feel a sensation as if your chest has been lifted and expanded (this should happen naturally, so do

This is the 'neutral' classical position that riders should adopt in the saddle. If you practise the above exercise frequently, the sensations you feel on the ground will become engrained in your mind so that eventually you will find yourself automatically taking up the same position when sitting on a horse. In this position, one should be able to draw a straight line from the rider's shoulder, down through the hip joint to the ankle – the often-quoted shoulder–hip–heel line (although in order for the rider to be perfectly balanced the line should pass through the ankle, not the heel). In practice, there will be times when, because of the movements of the horse or the requirements of a specific movement or exercise, this ideal shoulder–hip–ankle line will be temporarily lost; this is why I referred to it as a 'neutral' position. Even so, if you watch very good riders such as those of the Spanish Riding

not try to force it). Your arms should return to hang naturally by your sides, but they will be slightly further back than they were before the 'shoulder shrug'.

3. Maintaining this posture in your upper body, bend your knees slightly so that the angle between the rear of your thighs and your lower legs is approximately 105 degrees. This will vary according to the individual; the thighs should not be too vertical, and your knees should not be bent to the extent that you feel strain in your ankles. You should now feel securely balanced over your feet (if you do not, try adjusting the angle made by your knees until you do).

4. Finally, bend your elbows slightly and position your hands as if you are holding the reins.

Above: *This rider is demonstrating an excellent, well-balanced classical seat.*

Above left: *This is the neutral position the rider needs to assume in order to acquire a balanced seat. The model has brought her elbows a little too far back but she is very well balanced over her feet.*

Right: *The classical seat enables the rider to take responsibility for their own weight.*

School, you will see that even in the most demanding exercises their position in the saddle changes very little. Those are exceptional riders who have dedicated years to attaining this perfection of poise on horseback. Nevertheless, it is perfectly possible for riders of very little natural ability to become well-balanced, effective riders, simply by learning how to sit well on a horse.

Sitting crookedly

Most of us, although we may be unaware of it, tend to sit crookedly. We may collapse a hip (causing one shoulder to be higher than the other) or we may have a twist to one side. A test of this is to sit in a high-backed chair and see whether one of your shoulders is more in contact with the chair back than the other one.

Such rider crookedness cannot help but affect the horse's balance. Very often, riders complain that their horse is crooked when in fact it is the rider who is actually crooked! If your horse has a tendency to fall in or out of a circle on one rein, ask yourself whether this might be caused by your asymmetry. I know that my crookedness causes most of the horses I ride to fall in on the right rein and out on the left rein, and I have to make a conscious effort to counteract this. Fortunately, help with postural problems can be obtained via Alexander Technique and Pilates teachers (see page 154 for more information on both of these).

The importance of muscle tone

Adopting the correct classical position does not, however, mean that we should try to sit immobile in the saddle, like a statue. The rider who appears to be sitting still needs to make all kinds of minute adjustments, either to go with the movement of the horse's back or to influence her back by means of subtle muscular contractions in the rider's body. In order to have sufficient control of their own muscles to be able to make all these minor adjustments without introducing any involuntary movements, riders need to have a considerable amount of muscle tone.

Unfortunately, riders are often told that they must be so relaxed that they flop about on the horse. This not only prevents riders from being effective, but also creates a dead weight for the horse to carry – and, as anyone who has ever had to move someone who is unconscious knows, a dead weight is an extremely difficult burden to manage. Relaxation does not mean letting everything go – if we were totally relaxed, we would simply fall over. Relaxation in relation to what we do on horseback means a lack of tension in all but those muscles which are needed to

Left: Crooked rider: this rider has collapsed her right hip; as a result her right leg is shorter than her left leg, and her left shoulder is higher than her right shoulder.

perform a specific function, whether that function is to move limbs, maintain posture or send subtle signals to the horse through the contraction of certain muscles.

Riding from the centre

Some renowned teachers talk about concepts such as 'centred riding' (Sally Swift) or 'riding from the centre' (Sylvia Loch). Such concepts help us to understand how

Above: This horse is leaning on the bit and pulling his rider out of the saddle; the rider needs to firm up her position in order to influence him effectively with her back and seat.

the pelvis, along with the muscles of the abdomen and lower back, forms the 'command centre' of the seated rider. A secure seat based on good balance and firmly toned muscles in the pelvic area enables riders to use their hands and legs independently and with finesse. A floppy, insecure 'centre', by contrast, means that riders come to rely on their hands (which become harsh and unyielding as the rider uses them to hang on) and legs (which become stiff and ineffective as they tend to grip and clamp themselves against the horse's sides to compensate for insecurity in the seat).

Gripping with the knee can force the rider's seat off the saddle and make it ineffective, so clearly we do not want to encourage this. What is the alternative, if we want the rider to be secure in the saddle as well as being able to use the legs, abdomen and back freely? Some trainers suggest that riders should remain in the saddle by balance alone, but I know of no one who is not a trick or stunt rider who is actually able to do this. Most very good riders do something in order to remain glued to the saddle, even if they are not aware of doing so. Fellow of the British Horse Society Molly Sivewright (whose excellent books *Thinking Riding* parts I and II were reissued by J. A. Allen in 1999) suggests that riders think of 'gripping down' rather than 'gripping up'. This simply means that the rider firms up the muscles of the abdomen; not by sucking the stomach and abdomen in (which would create the opposite effect to what we want), but by bracing them in a way that supports the back and stabilizes the rider's position. The late Portuguese master of equestrianism Nuno Oliveira used to talk in terms of 'pushing the stomach towards the hands'. If you adopt the stance described in exercise 1 (pages 41–42) and breathe out vigorously, you will have some idea of what Oliveira meant. This simple action firms up the whole pelvic and lower back areas, and you will find you are still able to breathe freely.

So in considering what makes a good seat, we must start with the 'centre' and only then look at the outlying areas such as the hands, feet and – often overlooked, but of vital importance – the head.

The three-point seat

A great deal has been said and written about the so-called 'three-point seat' and there has been much debate about whether the 'third point' of this seat (the others being the two seatbones) is formed by the pubic bone or the coccyx. The latter, however, cannot come into contact with the saddle unless the rider's pelvis is tucked under to such an extent that riders adopting this position would cripple themselves with back pain within a very short space of

time. Sylvia Loch describes the three-point seat as follows:

> The expression 'three point seat' is one of imagery. It indicates a broad base of support represented by the entire pelvic floor rather than being isolated to the back of the seatbones only, sometimes known as a 'two point seat' ... Contact throughout this entire area leads to far greater support for the pelvis, the abdomen and ultimately the rider's spine ... (*The Classical Seat: A Guide for the Everyday Rider*, 1988)

Using the seat

However we describe the seat, riders are often mystified about how they are supposed to use it. In walk, sitting trot and canter, the seatbones simply 'go with' the movement of the horse's back – until we want to use the seat as an aid (as described in chapter 4). This is when the trouble starts. All too often, misled by what they are told by instructors, riders try to use their seat by simply tucking the pelvis under, flattening out the spine and grinding the seatbones down into the saddle (and, of course, the horse's back). Not surprisingly, horses tend to hollow their backs away from the resulting pressure and discomfort. This reflex action causes the horse's head to come up, the pelvis to flatten and the hocks to disengage. This version of the 'driving' seat has done so much harm that many instructors worldwide are now understandably reluctant even to talk about the rider's seat. As a result, countless riders are left knowing vaguely that they are supposed to do something with the seat, but having little or no idea how to do it.

The rider who knows how to use the seat correctly can use it to influence the horse's back without causing the horse to hollow. Sitting upright in the 'neutral' seat, simply brace the rectus abdominus muscle (see illustrations, right). This flexes the spine, flattening its contours slightly and causing the top of the pelvis to tip backwards a fraction. This pelvic curl is similar to one of the exercises prescribed for people with lower back problems. It is an essential part of the aids for asking the horse to halt, perform transitions and come into collection. Shifting the weight slightly more onto one seatbone will make the horse want to step sideways to rebalance herself under the rider; we will discuss the weight aids in more detail in chapter 4.

The thighs and knees

We tend to think of the rider's seat as consisting purely of the buttocks, but in fact, as Oliveira and many other great masters of horsemanship have pointed out, the seat extends down as far as the knees. This means that the thighs and knees are also an important part of the rider's seat. Riders are often told by instructors to take the knee away from the saddle; this is a misguided attempt to stop the rider gripping with their knee and thigh. Taking the knee away from the saddle prevents the rider from taking weight down the thighs; it destabilizes the seat and concentrates the rider's weight on the seatbones. Let's think about this for a moment. In scientific terms, the rider's body weight is a force acting on the horse's back. Pressure is the amount of force acting over a given area (pressure = force ÷ area). It follows from this that the larger the area, the less pressure will be exerted. So if the rider's weight is distributed over a large area (such as the seatbones, the fleshy parts of the

Right: *The rider's thigh should be in close contact with the saddle, as it is here.*

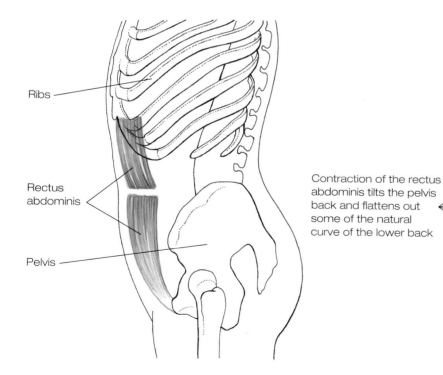

Ribs

Rectus abdominis

Pelvis

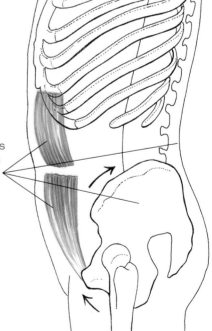

Contraction of the rectus abdominis tilts the pelvis back and flattens out some of the natural curve of the lower back

Above: *Bracing the muscles of the abdomen.*

buttocks and the crotch and the inner thighs down to the knee), the amount of pressure brought to bear on the horse's back will be very much less than if the weight is concentrated over a very small area (that is, the seatbones alone plus a very small area of surrounding flesh). The latter would be very uncomfortable indeed for the horse

and could even result in injury. The fact that the rider is separated from the horse by the saddle is immaterial; the pressure is still felt by the horse's back. We are always being told that a saddle should be constructed so as to distribute weight over a large area. Does it therefore not make sense to follow the same principle with regard to the rider's seat?

We can achieve a close contact of the thigh with the saddle without gripping either with the thigh itself or the knee; this involves really opening up the hip joints.

Exercise 2

This exercise is best carried out when actually mounted, although you can practise it while sitting on a saddle supported on a saddle stand. You really need the saddle to be on a horse, however, to feel just how wide apart the thighs need to be and how much your hip joints need to open up. If you are trying this exercise from horseback, have someone hold your horse in case she moves while you are mid-exercise.

With your feet out of the stirrups, take your whole leg as far away from the saddle as possible, opening the hip joint as far as you can without actual strain (this may feel rather uncomfortable at first). Rotate the upper leg inward slightly at the hip joint (this is a ball-and-socket joint, so it is perfectly capable of being rotated like this), then gently bring your whole leg back down so that the thigh lies snugly against the saddle. Carry out the same exercise with the other leg. You should find that because you have rotated your thighs inward slightly in this way, your feet will now be pointing more or less straight forward (depending of course on the individual rider's conformation as well as the shape of the saddle's knee rolls). In this way the entire leg is now in the most effective position to influence the horse, as well as providing security without the need for gripping.

Left: In order to achieve a close contact with the saddle without gripping, the rider needs to really open up the hip joint as shown in this exercise. This horse is very placid and will stand still during such an exercise, but if you are not sure whether your horse will do so, it might be best to have someone hold him while you try the exercise for yourself.

The rising trot and use of the thighs and knees

Most riders would probably agree that they find the sitting trot difficult to master, but comparatively few consider that they have any difficulties with the rising trot (posting); after all, it's something that is taught even to beginners, isn't it? Yet a correct rising trot, ridden in such a way that it helps the horse rather than hindering her, actually requires a great deal of precision and physical self-control on the part of the rider. All too often we see an approximation of a rising trot, in which riders bump up and down, pushing hard against the stirrups and hanging on to the reins in order to heave their bodies out of the saddle. In this kind of rising trot, the rider's lower leg is usually unsteady, swinging forwards as he or she pushes against the stirrup. Then, as the unbalanced rider – unable to control his or her body weight – thumps back into the saddle, the lower leg swings back and up against the horse's side. The lack of stability is reflected in the hands, which usually bob up and down, creating an unsteady contact with the horse's mouth.

This type of rising trot is most commonly seen in riders whose position fixes their lower leg too far forwards to begin with, or who have taken their knees away from the saddle in the manner described earlier. Classical trainer Charles de Kunffy says, 'When posting, do not stand up, "kneel up".' I think this is an excellent way of describing how the rider needs to think of the rising trot. If the knee is used as a pivot, and the rider 'kneels up' as Charles de Kunffy suggests, with the thighs firmly against the saddle (if the muscles are sufficiently toned, there is no need to grip), the rider rises forwards (not up and down as is so often seen) over the pommel of the saddle. The support of the thighs means that he or she can then return *lightly* to the saddle without thumping on the horse's back. The lower leg will remain still, as will the rider's hands.

An excellent way of developing the necessary strength in the muscles at the front of the thighs is to practise the rising trot without stirrups. This should be practised only in a safe, enclosed area, and preferably with the horse being lunged by a competent person, allowing the rider freedom to concentrate on his or her position. It will make the thigh muscles ache to begin with, and should be practised for only brief spells until the muscles become stronger.

Top: *Instead of using their thighs and knees to rise over the pommel, riders often push against the stirrups to lift themselves straight up out of the saddle.*

Above: *The riding trot: when the rider is no longer balanced over his or her feet, it will be very difficult to avoid landing heavily on the horse's back on returning to the saddle.*

49

The lower leg

Gripping with the lower leg is even worse than gripping with the thigh and knee because, as we saw in chapter 2, it will affect the horse's ability to breathe as well as making it very difficult for the rider to use the lower leg effectively. The lower leg should simply rest gently against the horse's side, ready to act when necessary.

The feet

The feet should, as far as the rider's individual conformation allows, hang roughly parallel to the horse's sides. If the leg is turned inwards at the hip joint as described earlier, rather than simply by forcing the toes in, the feet will naturally tend to fall into the correct position.

Too many riders make the mistake of ramming their feet home in the stirrups in an attempt to gain more security; however, this results in a stiffening of the ankles.

Below: The lower leg should simply rest gently against the horse's side, ready to act when necessary. If the leg is turned inwards at the hip joint, the feet will naturally tend to fall into their correct position.

Top: In a good rising trot, the rider rises forward over the pommel of the saddle and returns lightly to the saddle without thumping on the horse's back.

Above: A rising trot without stirrups can help to develop the muscles at the front of the rider's thighs.

This may not be such a bad idea when riding over jumps or across country, but for schooling on the flat the lower leg must be able to act with finesse at all times, which it cannot do if the ankles are stiffened in this way. The stirrup supports the ball of the foot just behind the toes; Charles de Kunffy tells us that, 'The stirrup is a small shelf on which you gently rest your toes.' If the seat is firm and balanced, this position of the foot actually gives the rider more, not less, security.

In spite of the fact that we are constantly being told that the heels should be down, forcing the heel down stiffens the calf and pushes the lower leg forwards. Until the hamstring muscles at the back of the thigh have stretched sufficiently to allow the heel to drop naturally, it is far better to ride with the heel level (but not raised – the heel should never be higher than the toe).

The hands and arms

Modern trainers often teach riders to hold their hands wide apart. The classical teaching, however, is that the hands should generally remain close together; the traditional advice is that they should be separated by no more than the width of the bit. There is a good reason for this. To discover what it is, first of all try these exercises, which can be carried out on the ground, but are most effective in the saddle.

Exercise 3

Let your upper arms hang by your sides, with your shoulders back and down, and your elbows close to your waist (how close will depend on a person's individual conformation; don't force your elbows in, just let them hang loose). Bend your elbows slightly and, without thinking too much about what you are doing, position your hands as if you are holding the reins. Most people will find that their hands automatically end up between 10 and 15 cm (4 and 6 in) apart. In this position the hands – or more properly the fingers – can be used with great subtlety and precision. The fingers can close or open on the rein as required; the whole hand can be rotated slightly at the wrist to indicate a change in direction or to give and take (see the photographs on pages 51–52).

Now try widening your hands until they are at least a foot apart. Immediately this increases tension in both the upper and lower arms. The hands and fingers can still be

Above: In this position the hands - or more properly the fingers – can be used with great subtlety and precision.

Below: The hand can be rotated outwards slightly to indicate a turn – sometimes known as 'leading the way with the thumb'.

There *is* a place for widened hands, as we shall see in chapter 6 when we come to look at encouraging the horse to relax and lower her head. This hand position should be used only temporarily and for that specific purpose, however, and never as a general way of riding.

Renowned classical trainer Charles de Kunffy has this to say on the subject: 'Riders with a wide hand position, as though holding the handle bars of a bicycle and steering about the horse's face, cannot gymnasticize and supple a horse.' And as one of the greatest riders of the twentieth century, the late Dr Reiner Klimke used to say, 'Hands together! Hands together unites the horse!'

The upper arms should be allowed to hang freely from the rider's shoulders, not held away from the body (elbows

Above: The rider can 'give' the hand forward slightly without moving the elbow: the hand is turned inward so that the knuckles are just visible from above. This eases the contact sufficiently for the horse to perceive it as a release. This should not be confused with the common 'pram-pushing' hands (with knuckles facing upwards) which result in a harsh contact; the turn of the hand is slightly exaggerated here to show the effect.

Right: Riding with the hands wide apart results in tension of the lower arm and loss of precision in the use of the hands.

used as described above, but much of the subtlety is lost because of the increase in tension. The action of the bit will also be affected; instead of receiving the precise, subtle sensations that can be achieved with the tiniest movements of the rider's fingers in the 'hands together' position, the horse will receive muddled signals via the bit. As a result many riders find themselves resorting to a strong contact, or pulling and fiddling with the reins, in an attempt to compensate for this imprecise communication with the horse's mouth.

out) or rigidly held in (elbows in). When riders are told by instructors to 'give' with the hands, there is a tendency to straighten the elbows and move the whole arm forwards. There is no need to do this – it will stiffen the arms and lead to a heavy contact with the horse's mouth. The elbows do not even have to move in order to allow the hand forwards quite considerably. When the reins are held correctly and the rider has established a soft yet positive contact, it is sufficient to rotate the hand slightly as shown in the photograph on page 52.

Above: Riding with the arms straight stiffens them and leads to a heavy contact with the horse's mouth.

Exercise 4

Let your upper arms hang by your sides with your shoulders back and down and your elbows close to your waist, as in exercise 3. Feel how relaxed your shoulders and upper arms are: in this position you can give minute, very subtle signals down the reins. Now move your hands forwards, straightening your elbows as you do so. You will immediately feel tension in your shoulders, and – if you are sitting on a horse – the weight of your arms will affect your ability to sit upright and firmly in the saddle.

with their hands and arms, which is not only ugly, but can actually have the opposite effect from what is intended.

If you watch videos of great riders such as Arthur Kottas, former First Chief Rider of the Spanish Riding School (and indeed of riders of the Spanish Riding School in general), you can see that their hands appear to be very still no matter what gait they are riding in. This does not mean that their hands are hard and unyielding; if they were, the horses would be unable to move with the fluid grace we

Above: *Holding the reins in a clenched fist will tense the lower arm and result in a harsh contact.*

Right: *The rein should be held firmly between the forefinger and thumb, with the latter making a little 'tent'.*

If you try to hold the reins by closing your fist tightly, and gripping the rein hard between the little finger and the third finger, this will tense the muscles of the forearm, which has the same effect as widening the hands or straightening the elbows. Instead, the rein should be held firmly between the forefinger and thumb, with the latter making a little 'tent'. The rest of the hand can then be soft and relaxed, ready to send the subtlest of signals down the reins, or do nothing – depending on what is required.

Fixed hands or following hands?

As the horse's head moves forwards and backwards in walk and canter, riders are often told that they must follow this movement with their hands in order to avoid jabbing the horse in the mouth. This often results in riders 'rowing'

are accustomed to seeing with such riders on their backs. So if we don't follow the horse's head with our hands, what can we do in order to avoid restricting the horse?

Nuno Oliveira used to say, 'Follow the horse's head with your back, not your hands.' As the horse's back is connected to her neck, this means that, as the head and neck move, so, too, does her back. If, as described earlier, we keep our elbows close to our sides, effectively they become part of the rider's seat. If the seatbones go with the movements of the horse's back, then so will the hands –

they will automatically follow the movement of the horse's head without having to be moved independently of the seat.

The head

One of the most important components of the rider's position is his or her head, yet this is often overlooked. Why is it so important? The human head weighs, on average, approximately 4.5–5 kg (10–11 lb). For someone weighing 63.5 kg (140 lb), this equates to around 8 per cent of body mass. Earlier in this chapter we talked about the effect an unbalanced rider has on the horse, so think of the potentially unbalancing effect of the heavy human head if the rider inclines it to one side or the other. Even riding with the head lowered to the front can put the horse more on her forehand, while many horses are hampered when jumping because their riders are looking down to one side.

On the other hand, the rider's head can be used as a weight aid. Good instructors tell their pupils to look between the horse's ears, or to look in the direction of a turn, because this will cause a shift in the rider's weight in that direction. As we have seen, the horse will naturally want to move in the direction of that weight in order to rebalance herself. In some very sensitive, highly trained horses, a slight change in the position of the rider's head can have a remarkable effect. Waldemar Seunig, a great horseman who studied horsemanship at the Cadre Noir at Saumur and at the Spanish Riding School in Vienna, wrote in 1941 that he had ridden Lipizzaner stallions at the Spanish Riding School who were so sensitive that a mere inclination of the rider's head to one side was enough to make the horse depart from a walk to a gallop towards that side.

Fitness and toning the muscles

It will be clear by now that many problems arise in riding simply because riders are not fit and have insufficiently toned muscles. How can this be remedied? There are countless ways of becoming fit and gaining muscle tone. How to get fit is something best discussed with your doctor because every individual will need a slightly different

Above: *Looking down can unbalance the horse.*

approach, depending on their body type and current state of health. Martial arts training (especially aikido) can greatly benefit riders because it teaches disciplined body movements, balance and muscular control. I also thoroughly recommend *Flexibility and Fitness for Riders* by Richenda van Laun and Sylvia Loch (2000).

Understanding the correct position is one thing, but how do we use it? The next chapter looks at the nature of the aids, and describes in more detail how the rider's position can influence the horse.

The language of aids

The aids are the physical means by which the rider communicates with the horse from the saddle and informs him what the rider wants him to do.

What is an aid?

In the seventeenth and eighteenth centuries, the English equivalent was 'helps', a direct translation from the French *aider*, which means exactly what it says: to aid; to assist. The idea was – and still should be – that the rider *aids* the horse to carry out their requests, rather than simply commanding him. Unfortunately, the original meaning seems to have been lost nowadays, so that when most trainers and riders (and certainly most behavioural scientists, even on the relatively rare occasions when they are themselves trainers and riders) refer to the 'aids', they mean cues that the horse has to be taught.

Conditioned cues and reinforcers

We can certainly teach horses virtually anything they are capable of doing by using learned cues. When the subject (a human, horse or other animal) performs an action that has a certain consequence, the nature of this consequence may increase the probability that the subject will repeat the action that led to it; this is known as a 'reinforcer'. If the consequence increases the probability that the subject will *not* repeat the action, this is usually known as a 'punisher'. So if little Billy tidies his room and his mother rewards him with something he likes or wants, this increases the probability that he will tidy his room again in the future. If, however, he kicks a football when he has

Below: *Negative reinforcement.*

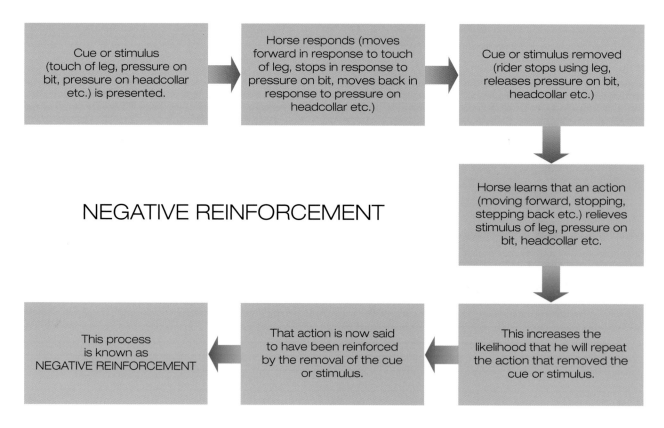

NEGATIVE REINFORCEMENT

Cue or stimulus (touch of leg, pressure on bit, pressure on headcollar etc.) is presented.

Horse responds (moves forward in response to touch of leg, stops in response to pressure on bit, moves back in response to pressure on headcollar etc.)

Cue or stimulus removed (rider stops using leg, releases pressure on bit, headcollar etc.)

Horse learns that an action (moving forward, stopping, stepping back etc.) relieves stimulus of leg, pressure on bit, headcollar etc.

This increases the likelihood that he will repeat the action that removed the cue or stimulus.

That action is now said to have been reinforced by the removal of the cue or stimulus.

This process is known as NEGATIVE REINFORCEMENT

Horse offers a behaviour (or behaviour occurs naturally) for example, moving forward, stepping back etc.

Immediately the behaviour occurs, the trainer gives the horse something he likes or wants (food, a stroke or a scratch etc.)

This addition of something desirable acts as a reinforcer, increasing the likelihood that the horse will repeat the behaviour.

POSITIVE REINFORCEMENT

A conditioned reinforcer can be introduced, for example when lunging or riding. This can be something like use of the voice or a clicker.

These processes are elements of POSITIVE REINFORCEMENT

This pairs the word(s) or sound of the clicker etc. with whatever is pleasant for the horse. He then associates the marker with something pleasant to follow later.

The trainer gives the horse something he likes or wants, while uttering a word (or words, although one word is best as it is more precise) or giving a click or other marker.

been told not to and breaks a window, his mother may take some of his toys away or prevent him from doing something he wants to do. In theory, this punishment should make Billy less likely to break windows in the future, but, as any parent knows, this does not always work. Punishment is not an effective method of training humans or animals because it can act only to *decrease* the likelihood of the subject repeating an action; it cannot *increase* the likelihood that the action will be repeated.

Top: *Positive reinforcement.*

Above right: *The trainer uses body language to ask the horse to step back.*

Right: *The horse starts to comply; as he steps back, the trainer will stop using the body language which asks the horse to move away. This is a very mild use of negative reinforcement.*

Reinforcement can work by taking something away (negative reinforcement) or by adding something (positive reinforcement). Some books and magazine articles give the impression that negative reinforcement is a form of punishment and always unpleasant, but this is misleading. With horses, negative reinforcement could indeed be something unpleasant, such as strong pressure on the bit, or it might consist of a very mild pressure, such as a light touch of the rider's leg. Another, very common example might be asking the horse to step back by means of

Left: This colt is being reintroduced to a halter following an accident. As he allows the trainer to slip the noseband over his nose, his compliance is reinforced by a small amount of feed, making this a pleasant rather than a stressful experience.

Below: Having worked well, this horse is being rewarded with a stroke on the neck.

backward pressure on the headcollar. Immediately the horse complies the pressure is released; this is the reinforcer. It is perfectly possible to use negative reinforcement in a way that is neither unpleasant nor oppressive. Positive reinforcement works by introducing something that the subject wants or likes; in the case of horses this could be a food treat, a scratch or a rub, or anything else that that particular horse finds rewarding.

Whether we are using positive or negative reinforcement, we need to get the timing absolutely right, or the horse may learn the wrong thing or even nothing at all. For example, if the horse steps back and you reward him once he has stood still again, you have actually reinforced standing still, not stepping back. The reinforcer must be given as the action takes place or the horse will not make the connection. The same applies to negative reinforcement: if we do not release pressure on the bit or the headcollar at the right time, the horse will not understand exactly what action produced the release.

Teaching cues

We make use of conditioning whenever we teach a horse to do something such as standing still, moving forwards when being led, stepping back, moving over in the stable, and so on. A cue (which could be anything we choose – for example, a tap on the shoulder or a verbal cue) is paired with an action (say a transition to trot or canter) and, when the horse makes the correct response, this is reinforced. So suppose we want to teach the young or green horse to trot on the lunge. We can wait until the horse decides to trot of his own accord (which he may well do if he is lively) or we can encourage him to trot by making a noise ('Shhhhh!!!' is always a good one) or trailing a lunge whip behind him. At the very moment he goes to trot, we say, 'Trot on!' (or whatever we decide to use as a cue). But how do we reinforce the horse's response? We can't get to him in time to reinforce the transition to trot, therefore he won't know exactly what he has done right. So we can do what many people do without realizing it: we use what is called a 'conditioned reinforcer'. For example, many people now use a clicker as a marker to signal when an animal has performed the correct action. The clicker is associated with a positive reinforcer of some kind (food, a scratch or a stroke, or whatever the animal likes), so that eventually the animal learns that the sound of the clicker means that

Top: *The clicker is a very useful 'marker' to indicate where the horse has performed the correct action.*

Above: *Before we can use the clicker as a marker it must first be paired with something the horse likes and wants, such as food, a stroke or a scratch. This young filly is being given a small amount of her favourite food.*

something good will be forthcoming. The conditioned reinforcer does not have to be a clicker; it can be a word or phrase, or anything that can easily be used as a marker. Conditioned reinforcers of this kind are especially useful when the trainer has to work at some distance from the animal and so cannot give the usual reinforcer in time; we can see how useful they can be to the trainer working the horse on the lunge, or to riders, who can then give the reinforcer at the correct moment. Having reinforced the response to the cue, we can then use the cue to ask for the action to which it relates. So when we say 'Trot on!' (or whatever), the horse knows what he is being asked to do because it is that response which brought him the reinforcer.

Trial and error

Many trainers insist that, where ridden work is concerned, horses learn by trial and error. Say, for example, the rider wants the horse to walk on. He has no idea what the leg aid for walking on means; it is just meaningless pressure on his side. If the rider uses the leg aid positively enough, however, the horse may move just to get away from the pressure. The rider removes the leg pressure and this is the reinforcer (some riders may also introduce something the horse likes as a positive reinforcer). The rider either ignores an incorrect response or (depending on the school of thought to which the rider subscribes) punishes it. If you think about it, the use of punishment is illogical in this context: if the horse does not know what he is supposed to do, he will

not understand what he is being punished for, and he will still not understand what he is supposed to be doing. After a number of repetitions (which may be few or many, depending on the individual horse), the horse associates the cue (the leg pressure) with moving forwards (which gains him release from the pressure and/or a positive reward of some kind). He therefore learns to move forwards when the rider applies leg pressure.

As Sara Wyche points out in *The Anatomy of Riding* (2004), this trial-and-error system is actually extremely inefficient. Not only is a lot of time wasted filtering out incorrect responses, but it is also extremely frustrating for both horse and rider if the former cannot work out what is wanted.

Left: This green young colt has no idea what the trainer wants him to do; he has to rely on the trainer's body language to give him clues. We would not normally work this close to the horse in lunging; the exception is when we are first starting a horse off on the lunge and we need to help him to understand what we want.

Above: The colt goes to trot spontaneously; the trainer applies a conditioned reinforcer (in this case, 'Good!'), so that the colt knows he has done the right thing. In ridden work it is much more difficult for the horse to make the right response unless we help him by means of correct use of the aids.

We can certainly teach a horse any number of cues which will produce a given movement or sequence of movements, then memorize all these cues so we can give them as required. But this fragmented approach not only depends on the rider being able to remember all the cues and exactly how and where they should be given, but also places an enormous (and, to my mind, unfair) burden of understanding on the horse. Some gifted teachers are able to succeed with this approach because they have the ability to interact with the horse in a manner which produces the right responses without the rider necessarily being aware of what they are doing. But less gifted riders (and less gifted horses!) may struggle, using such an approach, to rise above mediocrity.

Fortunately, no matter what some teachers may expound, we do not have to proceed in this hit-and-miss manner. As Sara Wyche says:

> If we look at pictures of the really great riders (great, not competitively, but artistically) – Colonel Podhajsky of the Spanish Riding School, for example, or the Portuguese horseman Nuno Oliviera – we see them sitting quietly, their shoulders simply square with their horse's shoulders, their hips square with their horse's hips. They didn't learn to ride by throwing together some diverse ingredients of human movement and hoping it might make nouvelle cuisine. They studied the way the horse moves, and the way the horse uses his anatomy, so that they could allow their own movements to fall into line with his.
> (*The Anatomy of Riding*, 2004)

This is the key to riding: understanding how the rider's actions affect the horse. People who do understand this – whether consciously or by intuition – are able to ride horses trained in a different culture, on another continent, and get them to respond in ways that are not open to riders who rely solely on learned responses that have to be taught.

Chapters 2 and 3 gave us some insight into how this horse–rider interaction works. We have seen how horses respond to shifts in the rider's weight, and to pressure on certain points of his anatomy. Now we can begin to put this together with the aids and see how the latter can truly *help* the horse to use his body correctly under saddle.

Weight aids

To make a turn, ride on a circle, or to encourage the horse to step to one side, the rider sits centrally but advances the inside hip fractionally and steps slightly into the inside stirrup. The resulting small shift in the rider's weight will

Top: *The rider asks for the turn by turning his body and shifting his weight slightly to the left. He cannot use the reins to turn the horse as he is riding without a bridle!*

Above: *As the horse turns in response to the shift in the rider's weight, he is helped by the rider's outside leg which nudges him into the turn.*

make the horse want to rebalance himself in that direction. Bracing the muscles of the pelvic area will have a 'stopping' action, as it will inhibit the transmission of movement along the back muscles.

Leg aids

In chapter 2 we saw how the intercostal nerves lie close to the surface along the horse's ribcage and how the rider's leg, correctly used, stimulates the muscles of the thorax to contract, raising the horse's back and bringing the hind leg on that side forwards. Some horses may need to be sensitized to the touch of the rider's leg, but a lack of response is most often caused by incorrect use of the leg aids. As chapter 2 showed, harsh and/or prolonged leg aids can prevent the nerve impulses from being transmitted to the muscles and will effectively make the horse 'dead to the leg'. For the same reasons, gripping with the lower leg also prevents the rider from being able to give leg aids effectively.

So we should think in terms of brief, light touches with

Below: The rider's leg, correctly used, stimulates the muscles of the thorax to contract. The lumbo-sacral joint flexes; the hind leg also flexes and starts to come forward. In this photograph you can just see the faint line made by the contracting muscle.

the leg, which will stimulate the electrical nerve impulses that raise the back and bring the hind legs forwards. As I explained earlier in this chapter, riders who are truly 'centred' will be able to use their legs in this way because they will not have to stiffen the leg in order to remain secure in the saddle.

The 'control panel'

In her ground-breaking book *The Classical Seat* (first published in 1988 and still available), Sylvia Loch set out

Top left: *Using the leg here activates button A, the 'impulsion' button for all active work.*

Top right: *Button B is used by the outside leg for lateral work, turns, canter and rein back.*

Above left: *Button C: a touch here stimulates the muscles which extend the foreleg.*

Above right: *Button D is used for elevated work such as* passage *and* piaffe.

the idea of a panel of 'buttons' on the horse's side. Using the leg on the girth (actually, because the leg is bent, fractionally behind the girth) stimulates button A, the 'impulsion' button for all active work. Slightly behind button A is button B, used by the outside leg for lateral work, turns, canter and by both legs for rein-back. Just in front of the girth is button C; a touch here stimulates the muscles which extend the foreleg. Finally, there is button D, which lies behind button B and is used for elevated work such as *passage* and *piaffe*. (Bear in mind, however, that, as we have seen, stimulating the nerves too far back may tip the horse onto his forehand, so for most riders this 'button' is perhaps best left alone.) Chapter 2 showed us that this panel of 'buttons' does very accurately describe what happens when we stimulate the nerves at these points on the horse's body. The image of the 'control panel' is a good one to keep in mind – never forgetting, of course, that the horse is not a machine, but a living creature with a mind of his own.

Timing of the aids

When an aid is given is just as important as *how* it is given. For example, you may have been taught (possibly without any further explanation) that when the horse is in walk you should use your legs on alternate sides. This has to do with the timing of the aids. In chapter 2 we saw what happens when a horse moves his hind legs forwards in walk and trot:

- As one hind leg swings forwards, the gluteus muscle of the hindquarters and the longissimus muscle of the back lengthen. The horse's ribcage on the same side swings out of the way to allow the leg to come forwards.
- On the opposite side, where the hind leg is supporting the horse's body weight, the gluteus muscle and the longissimus contract. The horse's ribcage swings to that side.

The rider has to learn to feel what is happening and gauge the right moment to use the leg. In each stride, there is a moment when each hind leg supports the horse's body weight; the hip, stifle and hock joints flex, the foot pushes against the ground to propel the horse up and forwards, and the joints of the hindlimb extend again. As this happens, the back muscles on that side will also extend, and

the rider will feel a sensation as though the seatbone on that side has been lowered, while the seatbone on the other side will feel lifted slightly. It is when the back and gluteal muscles are fully extended that they will start to contract again in order to pull the hind leg forwards. If the rider touches the horse's side with his or her leg at that precise moment, the stimulation of the muscles and nerves will increase the contraction, flexing the hock to a greater degree and resulting in a springier, more elevated and yet forward-going movement.

This may sound complicated and rather tricky to master,

Above: Correct timing of the aids is essential. This rider is using her leg just as the horse's back and gluteal muscles, having lengthened, are about contract again.

but with practice it becomes easy to feel which leg is on the ground. This is especially so if you feel for the moment when the horse's back muscles swell on that side and the ribcage, which swings to the contracted side, touches the rider's leg.

When riding in trot on a circle, riders are usually advised to rise as the horse's outside shoulder is coming forwards, and to change the diagonal on which they rise when changing

Above right: On the circle, if the rider rises as the inside hind leg and the outer foreleg start to come forward, this allows the horse's back muscles to lengthen and the inside hind leg to move forward freely and step under the body more. The horse has raised his head here because he suddenly caught sight of the photographer!

The half-halt has several functions:

- It warns the horse that we are going to ask him to do something other than what he is already doing (for example, we might be going to ask him to move from a walk to a trot).
- It helps him to rebalance and gather himself up for the next action.
- The very action of giving the aids for the half-halt helps riders to reorganize themselves for the transition.

The aids themselves are very simple:

- As the hind leg on one side touches down and starts to flex (which you will feel by the way the horse's ribcage bulges to that side), briefly close your legs against the horse's sides.
- Brace the muscles of your abdomen and lower back: as we have seen, this slows the horse by partially blocking the transmission of hind leg movement.
- At the same time, close your hands lightly on the reins, again partly blocking the flow of energy from the hind legs. We do not want this blocking action to be too strong because we want the horse to maintain forward movement, so the whole half-halt lasts no more than a second or two.
- Allow again with the hands as soon as the flexed hind leg starts to extend again, and ride forwards.

the rein and also to change it regularly when riding on straight lines. If we think of the lengthening and contraction of the horse's back muscles just described, we can see that this is sound advice. On the circle, if the rider rises as the inside hind leg and the outer foreleg start to come forwards, this allows the back muscles to lengthen and the inside hind leg to move forwards freely and step under the body more. On straight lines there is of course no 'inner' hind leg or 'outer' foreleg, and this is why the rider needs to change the diagonal frequently when riding straight lines, especially if trotting for lengthy periods – say, when out on a hack.

The half-halt

The term 'half-halt' is rather misleading because it suggests that the horse is almost coming to a standstill. It is really more like a 'half-transition'; it will become clearer what I mean when we come to talk about transitions themselves.

The full halt

Some trainers who are fixated on the idea of teaching the horse everything by means of learned cues concentrate on teaching the halt by means of such cues. In the process they usually pay too much attention to the horse's mouth, without thinking about what is happening in his hindquarters. We can certainly teach a horse to halt by pulling on the reins (or, more subtly, by increasing pressure on the bit via the reins). When the horse stops, we are then supposed to release the contact, thus 'rewarding' the horse for stopping. Most horses will eventually get the idea, but this is a very hit-and-miss way of getting them to halt. Some horses will simply pay no attention to the increase of pressure on the mouth, but will keep plodding on, possibly

Left: If the aids for halt are not given correctly, the horse may simply fall into the halt.

Below left: When the horse halts correctly, he is able to stop more quickly and efficiently, as well as being ready to move off again immediately on being asked to do so.

on his mouth, he is likely to flop onto his forehand, grinding gradually to a halt rather than stopping cleanly and sharply, because nobody has asked him to do anything else.

On the other hand, if the rider asks him to halt in a more collected manner, he will not only be able to stop more quickly and efficiently, he will also be ready to move off again immediately on being asked to do so. Instead of simply falling into the movement, the horse will make a sharp, smooth and efficient transition.

The aids for the halt are very similar to those for the half-halt, except that the abdominal and back muscles are braced more strongly, to provide more 'stopping' power. The leg continues to ask for forward movement. The rider steps down into the stirrups, closing the knees more firmly against the horse's sides. Together with the bracing of the abdomen and back, this inhibits forward movement: the rider effectively stops going with the movement (think about what you do if you want to stop suddenly while running, and you will have some idea of how this should feel). At the same time, the rider puts a little more weight on the thighs and crotch, easing his or her weight fractionally off the horse's back to enable him to step under more. Finally the hand closes on the rein, but *does not pull back*; it remains closed until the horse has halted, then eases the contact.

To begin with, do not ask the horse to remain in halt for more than a couple of seconds; you want to keep him 'on the aids' during the halt, ready to move off again. Gradually you can increase the amount of time you ask him to stand still during the halt, but initially be content with a few seconds of halt in a good posture rather than ending up with a longer spell in a poor one.

Transitions

Along with half-halts, transitions are among the most valuable and effective tools we have for training the ridden horse. Correctly executed, transitions from one gait to

in the hope that someone will ask them to do something more meaningful. Furthermore, this method does not help the horse to halt in a way that avoids strain to his vulnerable forelegs. If asked to stop in response to increased pressure

another – or lengthening and shortening strides within a gait – will:

- improve the horse's balance and the rhythm of his strides;
- encourage him to seek a contact with the rider's hand;
- impart greater impulsion to his movement;
- increase longitudinal suppleness;
- enable the horse to engage his hindquarters more easily;
- allow him to collect more easily.

Good riders will ask for many transitions in the course of a schooling session, sometimes several in the space of a single minute. However, simply asking for lots of transitions is not sufficient on its own; we must make sure they are of good quality or there will be no benefit to the horse.

The benefits of transitions lie in the fact that, to execute them correctly, the horse has to rebalance himself – just as he does when you ask for a half-halt, which is why all transitions should be preceded by a half-halt. Instead of simply falling from one gait into another, the horse who has rebalanced and, to some degree *collected* himself, will be able to move smoothly from one gait to another.

Top: *The rider braces her back and abdominal muscles to slow the horse in preparation for a downward transition. Her elbows needed to remain flexed in order to prevent the horse from leaning on the bit during the transition; this horse likes to do this as it is easier for him than using his back and hindquarters properly.*

Above: *In spite of his tendency to try to lean on the bit during a downward transitions the horse has 'changed down' efficiently and is about to move into a nice walk.*

Left: *Instead of simply falling from one gait into another, the horse who has rebalanced himself will be able to move smoothly from one gait to another.*

As always, the rider needs to help the horse as much as possible. Think ahead to where you want to make the transition. This could be at a marker on the school perimeter, a fence post or, if you are riding outside an enclosed area, a tree, rock, telegraph or electricity pole, or any other natural or built feature. Just before the point at which you want to make the transition, give a half-halt. At your pre-determined point, either ride upwards into another gait (for example, from walk to trot, or trot to canter) or ride downwards (for example, from canter to trot, or trot to walk).

To ride an upward transition

- Slightly brace your abdomen and back by breathing out – 'pushing the stomach towards the hands' as described in chapter 3 (page 46), but rather more strongly.
- Ask for forward movement with light touches of your lower legs.
- Allow your hand forwards just sufficiently to allow the forward movement.

If the transition has been ridden correctly, you will feel the horse move up into the new gait with increased impulsion and elasticity.

To ride a downward transition

- Close your legs against the horse's sides, a little further back than if you were riding an upward transition or simply riding forwards.
- Brace your abdomen and back as described earlier.
- Take a little more weight on your crotch as for a full halt.
- Close your hands lightly on the reins.
- As soon as the horse steps down into the new gait, allow your hands forwards slightly to ease the contact.

Many horses will raise their heads and hollow their backs, as collecting sufficiently to move down into the slower gait efficiently is hard work for them. Eventually, if the transitions are ridden correctly, such horses will become stronger and will no longer feel the need to prop themselves up in this manner.

Moving sideways

Many riders will have felt frustration when trying to get their horse to move away from the leg, because instead of moving away he persists instead in pushing up against the

rider's leg. All kinds of explanations have been offered for this – some plausible; others less so. The most likely explanation is that given previously regarding squeezing with the leg: if the pressure on the horse's side is too strong and/or prolonged, the nerves will be unable to transmit their signals to the relevant muscles. Besides this, the pressure may be irritating the horse and so he tries to push it away – wouldn't you?

If you want your horse to move sideways, remember the effect of unilateral stimulation of the intercostal nerves as described in chapter 2: the horse will contract his side away from the stimulus. If at the same time you shift your weight slightly in the direction in which you want the horse to travel, he will naturally tend to move under that weight. The leg aid should be exactly the same as described earlier, and the other leg should be absolutely still. Otherwise the horse will be confused as to what he is being asked to do.

Slowing down and speeding up in trot

The rider can use his or her position to slow a rushing horse down in trot, or alternatively to speed up a lazy trot. Once the rising trot has been mastered as described in chapter 3 (page 49), using one's body to slow the pace or impart more impulsion becomes relatively easy. All the rider has to do is slow (or speed up) the rate of his or her rise, and the horse will regulate his pace in order to stay in balance under the rider.

Giving the aids properly involves great precision and concentration on the part of the rider. This means that we do not let our attention wander or allow sloppiness to creep in because we cannot be bothered. If you do feel like that on a particular day, you would be better off not riding at all under those circumstances. If an aid does not produce the required response, you may need to try again, not more harshly, but more briskly and positively – and then, when you get the response you want, *leave the horse alone*. Do not keep asking once you have received the response: let the horse get on with his job, without further interference, until it is time to ask for something else. And do not forget to reward your horse each time he does as you ask. As a great twentieth-century horseman, Captain Beudant, used to say, 'Ask much, be content with a little – and reward often.'

Opposite top: Unilateral stimulation of the intercostal nerves will cause the horse to contract his side away from the stimulus.

Opposite below: If the rider shifts their weight slightly in the direction they want the horse to travel, he will naturally tend to move under that weight.

Above: The rider's 'outside' leg needs to be still, as it is here.

Equipment used in training horses

AT THE Classical Riding Club Conference of 2006, held in November of that year, Paul Belton of Albion Saddlemakers (one of the world's leading saddlery manufacturers) stressed the importance of tack that fits correctly and is appropriate for the purpose for which it is being used. Discomfort from ill-fitting tack can have a potentially crippling effect on the horse's ability to perform athletically and is the root cause of many physical and behavioural problems.

The saddle

Nowadays a great deal of emphasis is put on correct saddle fit, and rightly so. Ideally, a saddle should be fitted using a flexible 'profile' which is moulded to the shape of the horse's back and withers. Good, truly knowledgeable saddle fitters who understand the use of such profiles are not always easy to come by, however, and so riders are well advised to gain as much understanding as they can of the principles of saddle fitting. Bear the following in mind when choosing a saddle:

- The saddle should be positioned well behind the horse's shoulder blade, so that it does not interfere with the action of the shoulder. A saddle that is placed too far forwards will not only interfere in this manner, but will also tip the rider back onto the horse's loins – the weakest part of the back.
- When correctly placed, the saddle should sit level on the horse's back.
- The saddle should be neither too narrow (which will pinch the withers and tip the saddle back towards the horse's loins) or too wide (which may press down on the withers and will tip the saddle forwards onto the shoulders). A saddle which is too wide may also rock backwards and forwards and side to side,

causing bruising. Most ill-fitting saddles, however, are too narrow rather than too wide.
- The panels must be flat and level, and the stuffing must not be uneven or lumpy.
- The gullet should be at least 64 mm (2 ½ in) and preferably 76 mm (3 in) wide along its full length.
- There should be at least 153 mm (6 in) clearance between the rear of the panel and the horse's loins.
- The stirrup bars should be aligned correctly – that is, they should be fitted symmetrically on the tree; otherwise the rider will be unable to sit evenly.

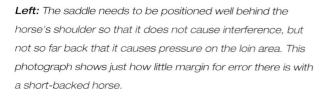

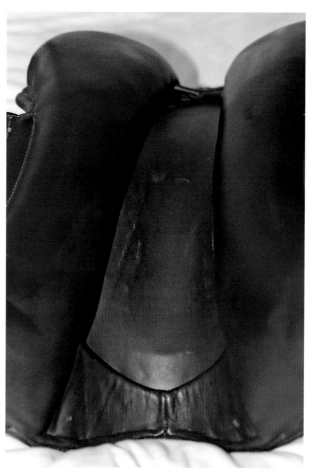

Left: *The saddle needs to be positioned well behind the horse's shoulder so that it does not cause interference, but not so far back that it causes pressure on the loin area. This photograph shows just how little margin for error there is with a short-backed horse.*

Top: *Here the saddle is placed too far forward; it will interfere with the action of the shoulders and, because it is unbalanced, may also cause bruising to the horse's back as it tips to the rear.*

Above: *In this photograph the saddle is too far back. In this position it will put pressure on the vulnerable loin area.*

Top right: *This saddle has ample width of gullet; ideally, the gullet should be the same width along its whole length, but in practice this is seldom the case.*

Saddles must fit not only the horse, but also the rider. Almost as importantly, they must be suitable for the type of activity in which horse and rider are taking part. This point is often overlooked, but saddle design can have an enormous impact on the rider's ability to influence the horse.

As most riders will be aware, saddles come in three basic designs (I am not including western or stock saddles here, as they are outside the scope of this book): general-purpose, dressage and jumping. As jumping (other than very basic grid work) is not covered in this book, I have concentrated on general-purpose and dressage saddles, with a brief glance at show saddles.

General-purpose (all-purpose) saddles

As the name suggests, the general-purpose (GP) saddle is the 'all-purpose' saddle chosen by the majority of those riders who do not wish to specialize in any specific discipline. The GP saddle is not so forward-cut as the jumping saddle, nor is it as straight-cut as a dressage saddle. A really good GP saddle can combine the best features of both the other types and in many cases will be the most sensible choice. All too many GP saddles, however, have the stirrup bars set much too far forwards. This means that, unless the rider is able to maintain a correct classical position regardless of the saddle, such forward-set stirrup bars will make it extremely difficult (and in some cases impossible) for the rider to maintain a balanced seat. The only way most riders could adopt the shoulder–hip–ankle alignment would be if they sat over the pommel, which is clearly not an option. Instead they will be forced into the unbalanced 'chair' seat described in chapter 3 (pages 39–40), which – as we have seen – drastically reduces the effectiveness of the rider's seat and lower leg.

If you are opting for a GP saddle, check the position of the stirrup bars. If it proves difficult to find one which fits you and your horse *and* has the bars in a position which will enable you to sit correctly for flatwork, it might be possible for a saddler to fit an extended stirrup bar to the saddle of your choice (or to a GP saddle which you may already own). Some saddles are made with adjustable stirrup bars such as those of the Wellep design; it is worth checking the internet for information about such saddles and where they may be obtained.

Dressage saddles

Many riders and trainers are of the opinion that, unless a rider is intending to compete regularly in dressage competitions, a dressage saddle is an unnecessary luxury. For schooling, however, a well-designed dressage saddle has many advantages over GP models. The straighter cut of the flaps (to accommodate the longer leg) and the placing of the stirrup bars so that the stirrup leathers lie in the centre

Left: A GP saddle is not so forward-cut as a jumping saddle, or as straight-cut as a dressage saddle.

Above: The straighter cut of the dressage saddle's flaps and the placing of the stirrup bars help the rider to achieve (and maintain) the classical position much more easily than a GP model would do.

Right: A jumping saddle has the flaps cut forward to accommodate the greater bend in the knee that results from shortened stirrups.

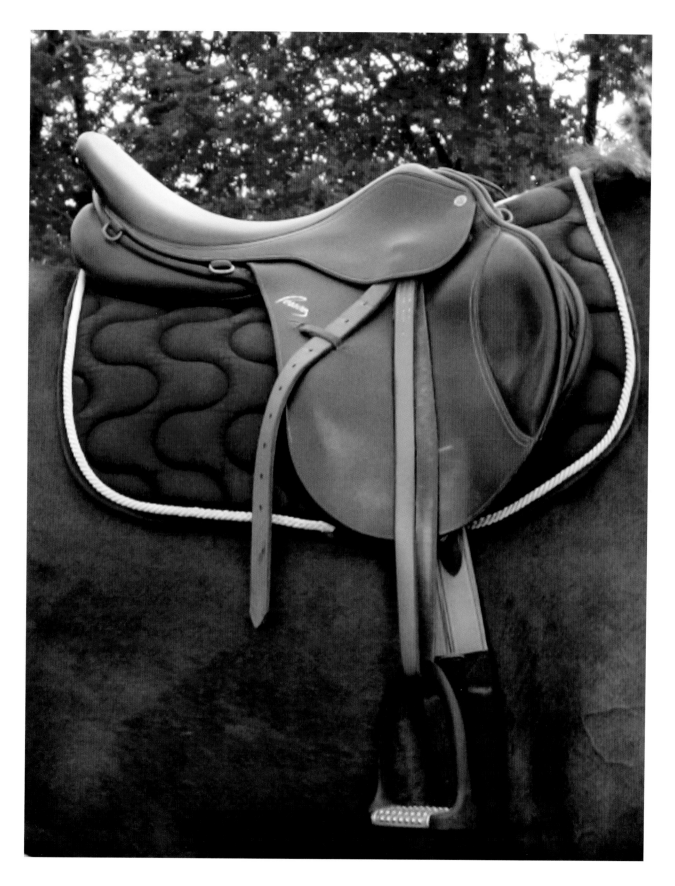

of the flap help the rider to achieve (and maintain) the classical position much more easily than a GP model would do. Many dressage saddles used to be designed with the stirrup bars too far forward, but the saddlery industry worldwide now seems to have addressed this fault, and there are now many excellent dressage saddles on the market. One design feature of many dressage saddles is rather puzzling: this is the cut-back head. This was originally designed for a horse with very high, knife-like withers, but the majority of dressage horses do not have this type of wither, so the continued use of this head remains a mystery. The cut-back tends to push the rider too far towards the cantle, when what we want is the reverse – for the rider to sit as far forward as is anatomically possible (this then puts the actual seatbones in the centre of the saddle). Some dressage saddles have slightly cut-back heads, which are less of a problem.

Show saddles

Some riders may find that a saddle designed specifically for showing may fit their requirements better than either a dressage saddle or a GP model, especially if they intend to do a lot of showing. Some older types of showing saddle had flat seats that were extremely uncomfortable and did not help the rider to maintain a correct position; many old photographs taken at shows depict riders sitting in an exaggerated version of the 'chair' seat because the stirrup bars were much too far forward (although some manufacturers did use an extended stirrup bar). Many of these saddles also had cut-back heads which, for the reasons described earlier, also tended to push riders into an unbalanced seat. Some saddle manufacturers, especially in

Below: *The cut back head tends to push the rider too far towards the cantle.*

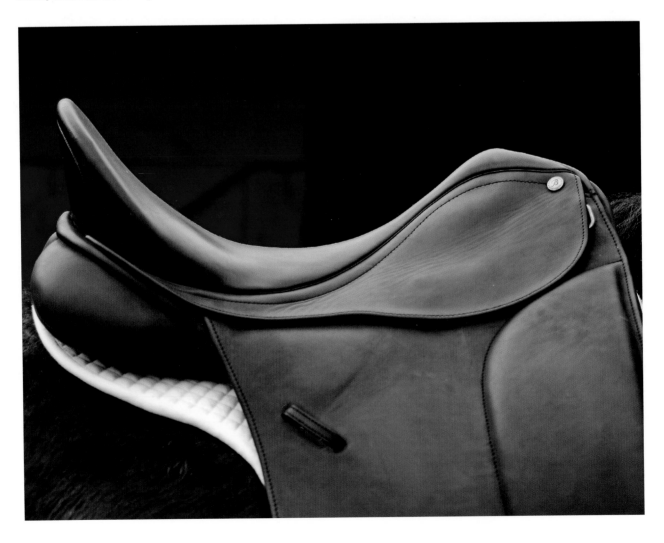

the United States, do still make this type of saddle; they are generally used by riders who take part in saddle-seat classes. The idea is that they show off the horse's front, but because of the way they are cut they are not suitable for schooling according to classical principles. So if you do decide on a showing saddle, make sure you go for the type that resembles a dressage saddle, but is not as deep in the seat and has normal-length girth straps.

Girths

Whatever type of girth you use, it should be soft and supple, and should not be placed too far forward, where it will interfere with the horse's elbow and rub the sensitive skin behind it. It should be fastened just tight enough to hold the saddle in place, and should be tightened very gradually. In some horses, especially sensitive types such as Arabians (who do seem prone to this kind of reaction), a

Below: A good show saddle can combine some of the best features of a dressage saddle with those of a good GP saddle. This saddle could be placed further back, as it appears to be interfering with the horse's shoulder. It sits up high so it may also be too narrow; however this could simply be a result of the way it is positioned.

Above: A well-fitting girth that spreads the pressure over a wide area. A girth should not be fitted too tightly or so far forward that it chafes behind the elbow.

sudden tightening of the girth can cause a shock to the system which results in a drop in blood pressure; the horse who goes down on her knees is actually fainting (vasovagal syncope). Some horses may react to the sensation with a panic reaction; this might take the form of backing up or even rearing (for more on this, see pages 139–40).

The bridle

The browband of the bridle should be wide enough to allow the headpiece to rest behind the ears without rubbing up against their base, and the throatlatch should be fastened so as to allow four fingers' width between it and the horse's

jaw. The noseband should not be fastened so high that it rubs against the prominent facial bones, nor so low that it interferes with the horse's breathing.

Above: A bridle with a cavesson noseband. I would ideally like to see the bit and the browband fitted a little lower, but there is plenty of room between the horse's head and the throatlatch and noseband.

Nosebands

Flash nosebands became very popular in the 1990s, perhaps as a result of the increase in popularity of dressage in those countries without any previous tradition of academic riding. More attention was being paid to the stillness (or otherwise) of the horse's mouth, and the flash noseband was supposed to stop horses from opening their mouths or crossing their jaws. There is nothing wrong with flash nosebands in principle, as long as the rider first tries to establish *why* the horse is opening her mouth (for more on this, see page 146).

The same cannot be said of the notorious 'crank' noseband, which has a strap which passes through a loop, then turns back on itself to fasten via a standard buckle. The idea is that the noseband can be fastened very tightly, so preventing the horse from opening her mouth. Unfortunately for the horse, this also means she cannot 'mouth' the bit in a way that will help her to relax her jaw;

Below: The flash noseband is acceptable as long as it is not fastened too tightly and is not used as a means of strapping the horse's mouth shut.

the resulting tension then passes all the way along the 'chain of muscles' to her hindquarters. The crank is thus self-defeating; its purpose is to mask a problem, not cure it, and it therefore has no place in the kind of horsemanship we are discussing in this book.

The bit

We rightly devote a great deal of time to the fit of a saddle, but not nearly as much to the bit. Yet the correct fitting of a bit can be as crucial to the horse's comfort as that of the saddle. Anyone who has had toothache, mouth or tongue ulcers, or an abscess anywhere in the jaw knows how the resulting pain can make it difficult to concentrate on anything. How often are horses expected to carry on and perform well when they, too, are suffering from pain and tension in the mouth and jaw?

Above: The crank noseband is self-defeating; its purpose is to mask a problem, not cure it.

The bit and mouth size

We all know that the width of the horse's mouth has to be taken into account when choosing a bit, but what about the rest of her mouth?

X-rays of a horse's mouth with the bit in place show just how little room there is in there for a bit. The tongue takes up a large proportion of the space available, especially if it is large and fleshy. The size of the muzzle itself is no indication of the size of the tongue. For instance, Arabians, who usually have comparatively small mouths, may have surprisingly large tongues, which, together with the narrow jaw, can make finding a suitable bit rather tricky.

I would strongly advise getting a qualified equine dentist to examine the horse's mouth, rather than trying to do it yourself; it is all too easy to get bitten, even when the horse does not set out to bite. Equine dentists use a proper dental gag which enables them to examine a horse's mouth in safety. If you are unable to find a proper equine dentist, most veterinary surgeons can examine horses' mouths competently, although as they are seldom specialists they may not be quite as good at it.

Measurements to take into account when fitting a bit are:

- the height and width of the palate – this affects the amount of space available for the tongue;
- the length of the bars in the lower jaw;
- the location of the canine teeth (tushes) in male horses and some mares – if they are quite close to the cheek teeth, this leaves less room for the bit;
- the space between the upper and lower jaw;
- the length of the mouth from the muzzle to the corners of the lips – this can be longer or shorter than the bars.

Right and below: Measuring the horse's mouth.

Measure the width of the jaw including the palate

Measure the length of the mouth from the muzzle to the corner of the lips; this may not be the same as the length of the bars. A horse with a short mouth may have long bars and vice versa

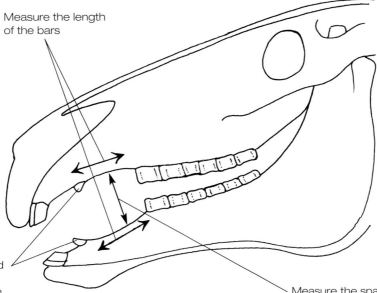

Measure the length of the bars

In male horses (and some mares), take note of the location of the tushes or canine teeth as these will affect the siting of the bit

Measure the space between the upper and lower jaw, including the height of the palate. Remember that the mouth has to accommodate the fleshy tongue as well as the bit

If the horse has a fleshy tongue which overlaps the bars when the bit is in place, the horse may try to get her tongue over the bit in order to relieve the discomfort. Sharp, narrow bars of the type found in many Thoroughbreds and their crosses, may be prone to bruising from a bit.

Once you have measured the horse's mouth and decided what kind of bit she needs, you will need to ensure that it is the right size and that it sits in the mouth correctly. In some countries it can be difficult to obtain bits that are narrower than 12.5 cm (5 in); the only alternatives often seem to be those intended for ponies. In the United States, it is usually possible to find bits of all types in a wide variety of sizes; this may reflect the fact that in the Americas, sheer size in horses does not seem to be of such significance as it is elsewhere. Fortunately the internet has made it possible to order bits from all over the world, so the lack of smaller sizes is no longer such a problem as it once was.

It is, however, an important point, because many horses, even those belonging to larger breeds, have proportionally much smaller mouths than one might suspect; it is not only dinky little Arabians who have dainty little mouths. If you are using a jointed snaffle, it is

Below: This bit is fitted so that it just lifts the corners of the horse's mouth without actually wrinkling it.

especially important that the bit is not too wide for the horse's mouth because the extra length of the mouthpiece cannons will make the joint rise up and bruise the roof of the horse's mouth. Too much width will also allow the bit to slide around in the horse's mouth, making precise communication difficult. On the other hand, if the mouthpiece is too narrow, it will pinch the corners of the mouth and create soreness. There should be just a very small amount of the mouthpiece visible on each side of the horse's mouth when the bit is in place.

The usual advice given regarding bit adjustment is that it should be high enough to wrinkle the corners of the horse's mouth. This can cause chafing, however, and may actually encourage the horse to try to get her tongue over the bit by way of relief. The bit should be fitted high enough to avoid banging against the canine teeth (in a male horse), but not so high that it creates noticeable wrinkles in the corners of the mouth. The best judge of where the bit should lie is the horse herself; when it is comfortable for her she will relax her jaw and gently mouth the bit – assuming of course that the rider's hands are polite!

What kind of bit?

Here, again, the best judge of what type of bit to use should be the horse; only she knows exactly how it feels. A simple jointed snaffle is usually held up as the most desirable bit for schooling, and many very good riders will do much of their school work with their horses in a snaffle, even when they reach advanced dressage standard. A single-jointed snaffle, however, is not always the best choice of bit. So much depends on the individual horse and her mouth conformation.

There is not sufficient space to consider all the different types of bit, or even all the available types of snaffle, so I shall look only at those bits of snaffle type which I have found to be most effective in schooling.

If you want to compete in dressage, you will be rather restricted in your choice of bit. At lower levels a snaffle is usually all that is allowed, and even then there may be certain types of mouthpiece and/or construction materials that are not allowed in competition; it is best to check with your national dressage regulatory body to see what the rules are with regard to tack used in competitions. Of course there is nothing to stop you from schooling your horse in one type of bit and competing with another; many horses

will accept this (I used to school my Arabian gelding in a soft rubber Pelham and compete in dressage with him in an eggbutt snaffle). Some of the Myler bits are now accepted by certain dressage organizations, and many horses who dislike an ordinary jointed snaffle will go very well in these.

Most other competitive disciplines place few if any restrictions on the type of bit used; as always, you should check with the organizations which set out the rules for specific disciplines.

The snaffle

If you decide on a single-jointed snaffle, choose one with a slightly curved mouthpiece, which relieves some of the pressure on the tongue and helps to prevent the bit from having too much of a 'nutcracker' action. The cannons of the mouthpiece should be solidly made and neither too thick (making them clumsy and less precise in the horse's mouth) or too thin (and potentially too severe).

Top: *The single-jointed eggbutt snaffle is one of the most popular snaffle bits. The rounded edges of the eggbutt help to prevent the chafing at the corners of the lips that often occurs with loose-ring snaffles.*

Above: *The French link snaffle is quite mild in its action; many horses go well in this type of bit. However, it does put extra pressure on the tongue so it needs to be used tactfully.*

A circumference of about 50 mm (2 in) at the widest point is not a bad guideline.

Many horses prefer a snaffle with two joints, as they are easier to accommodate than a single joint, especially in horses with small mouths. They do put more pressure on the tongue, however, which is generally very sensitive, so a two-jointed snaffle needs great tact on the part of the rider. The French link snaffle (see photograph on page 81) is a popular two-jointed snaffle which is quite mild in its action; many horses go well in this type of bit. It should not be confused with the much more severe Dr Bristol, with its angled centre plate (see photograph top left).

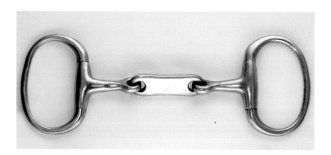

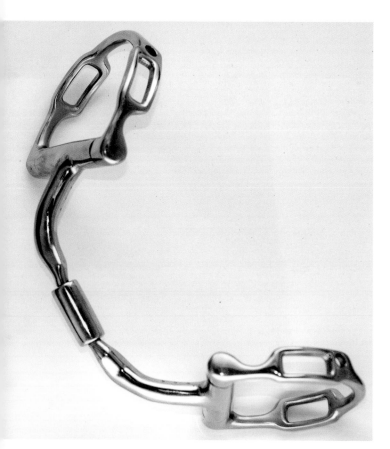

Myler bits

There are now all kinds of innovative bit designs, among them the Myler bitting system. Three of my horses go extremely well in Myler 'comfort' snaffles, which incorporate curved mouthpieces and centre barrels for tongue relief, independent side movement within the mouthpiece, and other features designed to encourage the horse to accept the bit without discomfort. The Myler system needs to be studied properly in order to understand how it works; see the Myler website – www.toklat.com/myler/home.html – for more information.

Bitless bridles

Some horses defy all attempts to find a bit to suit them. This may be because of their mouth conformation, or it may be because they have had previous negative experiences with a bit. In such cases you might want to consider going bitless. This would prevent you from competing in dressage and most showing classes, but you would still have plenty of other disciplines from which to choose.

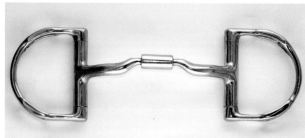

Above left: The Dr Bristol snaffle, with its angled centre plate, is more severe in action than the French link snaffle, with which it is often confused.

Above: Myler 'comfort' snaffles incorporate curved mouthpieces and centre barrels for tongue relief, independent side movement within the mouthpiece, and other features designed to encourage the horse to accept the bit without discomfort.

Left: This version of the Myler 'comfort' snaffle incorporates 'hooks' through which the cheek pieces and reins are slotted; this puts some pressure on the poll, which many horses accept very well as long as such pressure remains mild.

A bitless bridle can be just as severe in its action as any bit, however, so this should never be thought of as a 'soft' option. A horse's nose is extremely sensitive, so a rider who opts for a bitless bridle needs to have a secure seat and polite hands. You need to do some research before deciding whether this is an option that would suit your horse; I would recommend Elwyn Hartley Edwards's excellent book *The Complete Book of Bits and Bitting* (2004).

Gadgets

How do we define which training aids are legitimate pieces of equipment that can be used to the benefit of the horse, and which are simply 'gadgets', used by trainers and riders because they do not have sufficient knowledge or ability to obtain a result through correct work? At the Classical

Riding Club Conference referred to at the beginning of this chapter, Paul Belton of Albion Saddlemakers was asked, 'When does a piece of tack become a gadget?' His reply was: 'When you seek a piece of equipment to solve a problem that you created in the first place, then that equipment becomes a gadget.' I think this is a very good definition; the problem is that people generally are reluctant to admit that they *have* caused the problems they are trying to 'cure' with the aid of a piece of tack. This is where we need to be ruthlessly honest with ourselves: why do we feel we need to use a specific piece of tack?

Too often instructors urge riders to use training aids, either because the instructors have themselves been taught

Below: The effects of hollowing on the horse's muscles and spine.

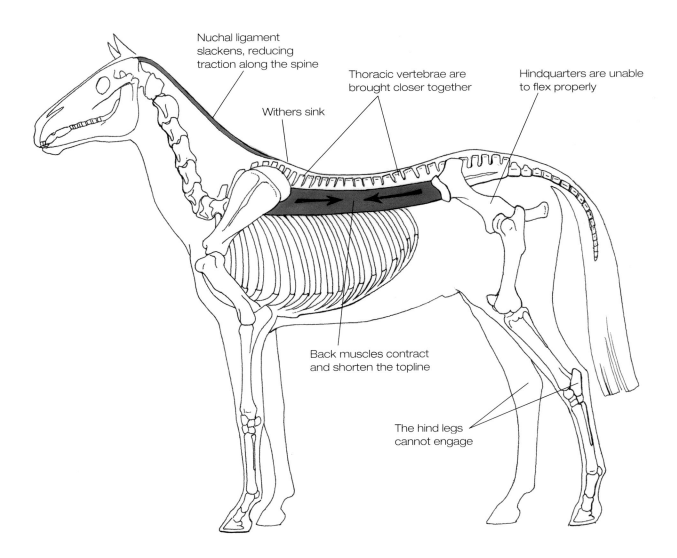

Nuchal ligament slackens, reducing traction along the spine

Thoracic vertebrae are brought closer together

Hindquarters are unable to flex properly

Withers sink

Back muscles contract and shorten the topline

The hind legs cannot engage

Above: *This rider is using draw-reins sympathetically. Few riders who use them are this tactful.*

to use them or because they do not know how to solve a problem by other means. The commonest reason for using training aids is to get the horse to go 'in an outline', and the training aid of choice is usually the draw rein or other tack which works in a similar way. This assumes that the horse can be taught to carry herself in the desired shape: she learns that in order to obtain relief from the action of the rein she must lower her head. This takes no account of the many reasons why horses come above the bit; it is neither the result of cussedness on the part of the horse nor a sign that she has not understood what is required. Horses do not actually enjoy going around with their noses poked and

their backs hollowed when carrying a rider. Apart from being uncomfortable, this posture stiffens the back and may result in the painful condition known as 'kissing spines'; this occurs when the spinous processes of the vertebrae touch as a result of the back being hollowed. As we have seen, one of the most common reasons for a hollow back is weakness of the neck. Another, perhaps even more common, is pressure from the weight of the rider. Unbalanced riders who do not take responsibility for their own weight in the manner described in chapter 3 will make the horse hollow away from the discomfort. This causes the back muscles to contract and shorten, bringing the head and neck closer to the croup along the topline and disengaging the hind legs.

Some horses in this situation will fight against attempts to make them lower their heads. Others will oblige and lower their heads, but their backs will remain hollow and stiffened, and the hind legs will be unable to engage.

Draw reins and other auxiliary reins do have their place, mainly in the re-training of certain horses, but they are seldom in their place – and in any case should only be used by extremely sympathetic, experienced riders who really understand the principles that underlie what they are doing. The photograph on page 84 shows a rider using draw reins sympathetically. The rider's hands are soft and giving, and she is not using the draw reins to make the horse lower his head. The reins will come into play only if the horse raises his head above a certain level; otherwise he is free to stretch forwards into the light contact. Unfortunately, few riders who use draw reins are this tactful.

One of the biggest problems with training aids is that they effectively come between the horse and the rider. They encourage the rider to stop paying attention to what the horse is telling them, and instead rely on a piece of tack to solve their problems, when what they really need to do is to understand the root causes of those problems and tackle them by using that understanding.

The real value of training aids

The time to consider using training aids is when working the horse (especially a green or novice horse) on the lunge in preparation for ridden work. Horses who are not burdened by a rider can run around with their heads in the air without doing themselves any damage because they do not have to accommodate a weight on their backs. So when they are first lunged prior to being ridden they are likely to move exactly as they do at liberty in the field. We want

Below: When horses are first lunged prior to being ridden they are likely to move exactly as they do at liberty in the field.

them to stretch forwards and down, and engage the hindquarters so as to strengthen the top and bottom lines, and it is here that correctly fitted side reins, or an auxiliary rein such as the Chambon or de Gogue, can really be of benefit.

Side reins

Some trainers use side reins as a matter of course, but as always each horse should be treated as an individual and, as with all training aids, side reins should be used only if the horse will really benefit from them. They may be especially useful for horses who, through lack of balance, have a tendency to turn their heads to the outside on a circle and fall onto the inside shoulder, especially in canter, as they can be adjusted so that the inside rein is slightly shorter

Below: Horses should reach forward and down on the lunge, engaging the hindquarters so as to strengthen the top and bottom lines. This mare has not quite achieved true engagement, but her head and neck positioning will help to free her back muscles. If she keeps moving forward on the lunge with impulsion, she will eventually be able to engage properly.

than the outside, regulating the amount of bend. Side reins may also be used to suggest to the horse that she lowers her head, but should not be used to tie the horse's head down or unduly restrict the freedom of her neck.

The Chambon

The Chambon resembles a kind of running martingale and is widely used in Europe, although it is less well known in the English-speaking countries. It is used in lunge work and is aimed at encouraging the horse to lower her head and neck. It comes into effect only if the horse raises her head above a certain level (which can be adjusted). It works by exerting a mild pressure on the poll; there is no backward force involved, and the Chambon does not prevent the horse from stretching her neck forwards.

The de Gogue

Like the Chambon, the de Gogue is named after the French cavalry officer who invented it, and it works in basically the same way. The de Gogue is more sophisticated and complex than the Chambon, however, and is potentially more powerful in its effect, as the action on the

poll is more direct. It therefore needs more tact than the Chambon. Unlike the Chambon, it can be used in ridden work, but I would advise anyone thinking of using the de Gogue to restrict its use to lunge work, as ridden work with this auxiliary rein is really the province of the expert.

With either the Chambon or the de Gogue, the person doing the lunging must ensure that the horse is moving forwards actively from behind. As long as this is the case, the activity of the hind legs together with the lowering of the head and neck will help to strengthen the top and bottom lines, as well as the muscles of the neck.

There are many other training aids available for which all kinds of claims are made – for example, that they will enable the rider to ride with softer hands as well as enabling

Above: This horse is being lunged in a de Gogue.

the horse to work in the proper outline. These claims should be regarded sceptically, because a rider who understands the correct principles of riding and training does not – except in some special circumstances – need such aids, and the rider who does not understand the principles has no business using them!

Ultimately, the best advice one can give with regard to tack of any kind is:

- Understand its function and effect.
- Make sure it fits.
- Keep it simple!

Improving a horse's athletic ability

BEFORE WE can achieve anything of value in our schooling sessions, the horse must first of all be calm and relaxed. As we saw in chapter 3, there must be a certain amount of tension in muscles actively engaged in movement or the control of posture. Excess tension, however, either in these muscles or elsewhere in the body, prevents the active muscles from performing their function efficiently, leading to strain and resulting pain and discomfort. This is especially the case if the tension originates in the mouth and jaw, because of the way in which the muscles in this area are linked to the muscles of the neck and back.

Tension and excitability may be caused by a number of factors:

Overfreshness If the horse has an excess of energy (whether from overfeeding or lack of exercise), he will be unable to concentrate and will be likely to indulge in 'high jinks'.

Solution Ensure the horse has adequate turn-out and/or exercise away from the schooling area. Feed according to work done; horses in light to moderate work may need no more than access to good forage. The type of schooling described in this book comes in the light to moderate category.

Above right: *This young Lusitano mare became rather exuberant at her first public demonstration.*

Right: *Ridden sympathetically, she soon settled down.*

Apprehension This may be caused by unfamiliar surroundings, or by something unfamiliar in familiar surroundings – for example, an object in the schooling area that would not usually be there. Horses may also be disturbed by sudden or intermittent noises, especially if they cannot tell where the sound is coming from.

Solution Before starting serious work, ensure that the horse is familiar with the schooling area (if schooling is carried out when riding out, let him become thoroughly accustomed to the route before asking him to concentrate on school exercises). Do not expect the horse to concentrate on work on windy days, as the sound of the wind will interfere with his ability to judge the direction from which noises are coming, which will increase his level of apprehension further. Try to locate and remove unfamiliar objects/the source of intermittent noises, and remove any other animals such as dogs or cats, unless the horse is familiar with them and does not appear to be concerned by their presence.

Fear Depending on the horse's past experience, he may be anticipating punishment for failure to perform according to the rider's expectations, or he may have been inadvertently punished by poor riding, inconsistent/incorrect application of the aids, etc.

Solution Use great tact when asking anything of the horse; allow plenty of breaks between exercises; reward often; and make sure there are no negative consequences for the horse if he makes a mistake. Be extra critical of your riding and ensure that you give the aids clearly, consistently and tactfully.

Pain or discomfort These can arise from ill-fitting tack; incorrect bitting; poor shoeing/foot trimming, lameness in fore- or hind limbs; pain or stiffness in the neck or back; poor rider position; or the rider taking up a harsh, unyielding contact.

Solution Double-check the fit of all tack and make sure that the bit fits correctly and is of the right type for the individual horse. If lameness in one or more limbs is suspected, have the veterinary surgeon and the farrier check shoeing/foot trimming, and if necessary seek a second opinion. Check your riding as for 'fear' previously, being especially careful that you are not inadvertently taking up too strong a contact.

There may be more than one cause of tension and excitability, and riders must evaluate the situation carefully, being especially critical of their own riding.

In all the exercises described in this and the following chapters, wherever the exercise or movement is to be ridden in trot, the rider should employ the rising trot (posting), as this will help to keep the horse's back free of encumbrance.

When schooling, keep sessions short and sweet; 20 minutes of good work is worth far more than an hour of poor or mediocre work. If a schooling session is not going well, do not persist; go for a ride in the fields or in the country instead. If what you are trying is not working, go back to something the horse finds easy. Always try to end on a good note, even if you have not achieved what you hoped for.

Warming up

Never expect the horse to work 'on the bit' at the start of a schooling session. No horse can work properly until his muscles have been warmed up by gentle exercise beforehand. As already noted previously, he also needs to be given the chance to look around him and take note of his surroundings, so that nothing in the environment will take him by surprise and cause him to take fright.

Start every session in walk on a loose rein. There is no point in setting off at a spanking trot, as so many people do, because until the horse is sufficiently loosened up and calm in his mind he is liable to become more, not less, tense. If the horse has already been introduced to shoulder-in, one very good way of warming up is to work him gently in hand for a few minutes (for more about the shoulder-in see chapter 8).

In-hand work

This type of work from the ground is not at all well known outside Spain, Portugal and academies of equitation such as the Spanish Riding School. This is a pity, as it is an excellent way of relaxing the horse, softening his back and gaining his attention. At the Spanish Riding School and in

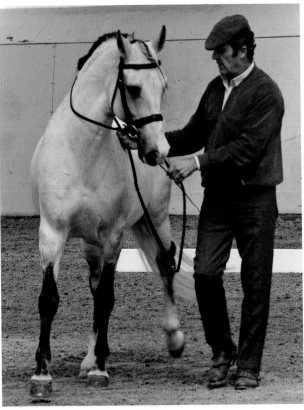

Above: *Don Francisco de Bragança works with Lusitano gelding Jeitoso in shoulder-in.*

Left: *Classical in-hand work is an excellent way of relaxing the horse, softening his back and gaining his attention.*

Spain, in-hand work is carried out with the horse wearing a cavesson, whereas in Portugal a simple snaffle bridle is generally used.

The trainer walks by the horse's side, holding the inside rein close to the bit, with the outside rein held over the horse's neck. The horse is asked to walk on, halt, rein back or perform a shoulder-in; these movements can be carried out either in a straight line (for example, along a fence or other boundary) or in a circle around the trainer.

You may find it helpful to do what a number of classical trainers do when working the horse in hand. They encourage him to bend around them by pressing his side at approximately the point where the rider's leg would touch him. This stimulates the intercostal nerves in exactly the same way as the rider's leg. It causes the horse to in-curve his side away from the pressure, at the same time raising his back and encouraging engagement of the hindquarters because of the effect of nerve stimulation on the horse's back and abdominal muscles. If he is then gently worked in shoulder-in, the joints of his hind legs will bend and consequently become looser and more active.

Until the horse has reached the stage where he can start work in shoulder-in, I would recommend in-hand work on straight lines, progressing to a little work on a simple circle around the trainer.

Exercise 1

Stand by your horse's shoulder, taking the inside rein in your left hand if working on the horse's left, and in the right hand if working on his right. Take hold of the outside rein where it passes over the horse's neck. Do not hold the reins too tightly, as you want to encourage the horse to relax, and if you have never tried in-hand work with him before he may be a little anxious about a strange experience. Ask him to walk on for a few steps, then halt. Ask for a few more steps, then halt again. Repeat this a few times until you feel the horse start to relax, then after the next halt ask for a few steps of rein back. All you need to do to get a response in most cases is to walk forwards yourself, and the horse will follow; in the same way, he will halt when you do, and will step back when you do. If he resists a little, this is nothing

Left: In-hand exercise 1: Sylvia Loch with Lusitano mare Andorinha.

Top: In-hand exercise 2: Sylvia Loch with Lusitano mare Andorinha.

Above: In-hand exercise 3: Sylvia Loch with Lusitano mare Andorinha.

to worry about; stay calm and relaxed yourself, and he will soon start to relax. If the horse starts to get a little excited, halt and wait until calm has been restored, then start again. Repeat this exercise on the other rein.

Exercise 2

First, carry out exercise 1, then ask the horse to walk around you in a small circle. You will start to feel him offering the beginning of some shoulder-in. Repeat this several times; however, if you feel any resistance beyond an initial tensing as the horse tries something new, do not be tempted to continue or the exercise will be of no value. Go back to the simple exercises, then try again. Eventually the horse will start to soften in his jaw, neck and back. Always end with a few steps in a straight line. Repeat the exercise on the other rein.

Exercise 3

Carry out exercises 1 and 2. As the horse starts to relax in the circle around you, ask him to move towards the outside track in shoulder-in, and, maintaining the shoulder-in position, walk up the track for three or four steps. Come off the track again and back onto the small circle, ending with a few steps in a straight line. Repeat the exercise a few times, then continue on the other rein.

Relaxation from the saddle

As suggested earlier, you should start each session by allowing the horse to look around him and accustom himself to his surroundings; this is a good idea even if you school in the same place every day. Start by walking on a loose rein. Some people are alarmed by the thought of this, thinking that the horse might run off with them, but this is

Above: *Once the horse feels relaxed enough, try a little trot on a loose rein.*

Left: *Start each session with a walk on a loose rein.*

rarely the case. Horses are much more likely to become tense and excitable if they are held on a tight rein because this naturally increases tension in the neck and back muscles. The late Reiner Klimke used to exhort pupils at his clinics to let the reins go – right down to the buckle.

If the horse is more interested in what is going on around him even after a few minutes of walking around, make lots of changes of direction, still in walk. Try some transitions from walk to halt and into walk again. Ride forwards six or seven paces, then halt. Ride forwards another six or seven paces, then halt again. The horse will then have to start paying attention to you and where you are asking him to go, rather than becoming distracted by things outside the school. You can tell where his attention lies by watching his ears: if they are pricked forwards, he is thinking about something straight ahead, not what you are asking him to do. The horse who is listening to his rider (in the sense of paying attention) will have his ears slightly turned back towards the rider.

After a few circuits of the schooling area in walk, if the horse feels relaxed enough, try a little trot on a loose rein. If you feel him start to tense up again, go back to walk until he is truly relaxed and paying attention to you. Some horses, perhaps less forward-going than others, may benefit from a little canter on a loose rein instead; this often seems to get such horses moving better than the trot.

The walk

I have emphasized working in walk to begin with because this is the best way to get the horse to relax. Work in walk also has other benefits. It is the best gait in which to warm up because it exercises more muscle groups than any other gait. From an active walk you can ride many of the exercises described in this chapter and chapters 7 and 8, which enables both horse and rider to reorganize themselves quickly if things go wrong.

Long and low

Throughout every schooling session, the horse should periodically be encouraged to stretch his neck right down. Maintaining a light contact, lengthen the reins and invite the horse to stretch down by widening the hands slightly and lowering them until they are resting on each side of the

withers. If the horse has been working correctly, he should follow the contact down (there should never be any suggestion of pulling his head down). If he simply pokes his nose or snatches the reins out of your hand, just ask for a more active walk and try again; vibrating the reins slightly often helps to suggest to the horse that he lower his head. The walk should in any case remain active; this is not an excuse for the horse to slop along on his forehand. As long as there is no suggestion of force, the very act of lowering his head will help to relieve any residual tension that might be causing the horse to poke his nose and/or snatch at the reins.

Trotting poles

Working over trotting poles is an excellent and very simple way of helping horses to regulate the rhythm and regularity of their stride. The poles themselves can be made of wood

Above: If the horse has never seen trotting poles before, allow him to look at just one pole on the ground.

Left: Throughout every schooling session the horse should periodically be encouraged to stretch his neck forward and down.

Right: Start with just one pole on the ground and let the horse become familiar with it until he is happy to walk over it without fuss.

94

or plastic. Wooden poles are likely to be cheaper and more readily available than plastic, but they tend to be heavy and clumsy. Poles made of plastic are much lighter and easier to move, and are less likely to hurt the horse and give him a fright if he accidentally catches one with his foot. Lighter poles are more easily knocked out of position, but this seems to me to be a minor inconvenience when set against the benefits. The usual length of trotting poles is around 3–3.5 m (10–12 ft), but this is only a guideline. They can be used flat on the ground or raised on blocks, cavalletti (see chapter 8, pages 124–25) or other solid supports. In this chapter we will be considering only poles laid flat on the ground; work over raised poles will be covered in chapter 8.

Work over trotting poles is beneficial in a number of ways:

- The horse has to lift his feet, thus increasing the activity in his hindquarters.
- In order to clear each pole in turn, he has to adopt a regular rhythm and length of stride.
- This helps to improve the horse's natural gaits.
- It also helps to develop and improve his balance and co-ordination.

When working over poles it is best, if at all possible, to have someone on the ground to help you with placing the poles and replacing them if any are dislodged. The spacing of the poles needs careful thought. If they are placed too far apart, the horse may strain his muscles as he tries to reach too far in order to clear them; unable to clear a pole, he may step on it and injure himself by slipping. If the poles are too close together, the horse may take mincing steps in order to get his feet between them, which again may result in strain; he may also step on the poles.

The best way to gauge how far apart poles need to be is to observe the horse in walk and trot, and see how many strides he takes between each marker in the schooling area. This will give you some idea of his stride length. Approximate distances for horses of medium size are:

In walk: 90–100 cm (3–3.4 in) apart
In trot: 120–170 cm (4–5.3 in) apart

Above: *Once the horse is happy to walk over the pole, take him over it in trot.*

Opposite: *Progressing to a row of poles, start off in walk.*

These are guidelines only and will vary depending on the size of the horse and his individual type of movement: a small horse with a long stride may need the poles to be further apart than a large horse with a short stride. Having someone on the ground to observe how the horse copes with the pole placement will help you to decide what distance adjustments need to be made; make them in small increments or reductions until you get the distance right. The aim is for the horse's feet to land approximately halfway between the poles, as this even distance will help to regulate his stride.

You can lunge a horse over trotting poles, but riding over them will enable you to guide the horse so that he approaches them head on and not at an angle, and that he goes over them in a straight line. Otherwise he is more liable to misjudge the distance and catch his feet. If he has never seen trotting poles before, lead him up to them and let him see them; some horses like to sniff at them as well. Start with just one pole on the ground, and either ride or

lead the horse over the pole from both sides until he is familiar with it and is happy to walk over it without fuss.

Introduce him to the idea of going over a line of poles by adding one pole at a time, to allow him to get used to the idea of lifting his feet over a series of poles. If you try to take him over several poles before he is ready, he may become anxious and simply blunder through them, possibly catching his feet in the process. This may put him off, so as with all exercises take your time. Start off in walk and, when the horse is going over the poles confidently and in a

Below: *When the horse is going over the poles confidently and in a good rhythm, you can adjust the distance and take him over them in trot.*

good rhythm, adjust the distance and take him over them in trot. Always use the rising trot, and allow the horse to stretch his head and neck forwards to help with his balance and also to allow him to see the poles properly.

Canter pole

A single pole placed across a corner of the school is an excellent way of helping the horse to find his balance in canter; it also helps horses to strike off on the correct lead.

Above: A single pole placed across a corner of the school is an excellent way of helping the horse to find his balance in canter.

Most horses accept work over trotting poles extremely well, and some seem to really enjoy it. There are others, however, who will try to rush over the poles in trot, and with such horses you will need to use your body to slow the trot down, as described in chapter 4.

Rhythm, impulsion and straightness

I N THIS chapter we will look at exercises that continue to promote relaxation and that will help to establish rhythm, impulsion and straightness. It may seem odd that so much of this work involves bending, especially on circles. How does this help the horse to go straight? And how does it help to establish rhythm?

As we have seen, horses often rush because they are unbalanced. Working on straight lines at anything faster than a walk will not help them, because it is easier to run on in a straight line than it is on a circle or while bending. So these exercises help to steady the horse and allow her to find her balance and natural rhythm. A horse who is relaxed and moving without constraint (that is, without being restricted by the rider or her tack) will be able to reach out and accept the contact with the rider's hands. The exercises will also have a suppling effect, which will help the horse to move straight. And finally, as a result of all this, she will develop true impulsion: the energy generated in the hindquarters will be directed into powerful, contained and yet free-flowing forward movement.

Before we go on to look at the exercises, let's think about the twin concepts of contact and outline, which many of the exercises described in this chapter will help to establish.

Contact and outline

In chapter 4 we talked about the infamous 'outline', and that this is something the horse produces, not the rider. As Udo Bürger says, 'Carriage is a consequence of balance. A body cannot hold itself up properly if it has not got firm muscles.' (*The Way to Perfect Horsemanship*, 1999.) So all the exercises described in this and the following chapters are designed to help the horse to relax, find her balance, move forwards straight and with impulsion, and strengthen her muscles so that she can carry herself properly. As all of these things happen, she will find it easier to flex the joints

'on the bit' actually has little to do with the bit and everything to do with what we have been discussing in this chapter regarding the horse's posture. The Fédération Equestre Internationale (FEI) defines 'on the bit' as follows:

A horse is said to be 'on the bit' when the neck is more or less raised and arched according to the stage of training and the extension or collection of the pace, accepting the bridle with a light and soft contact and submissiveness throughout. The head should remain in a steady position, as a rule slightly in front of the vertical, with a supple poll as the highest point of the neck, and no resistance should be offered to the rider. (FEI Rules for Dressage Events, 22nd edition, January 2006: Article 401, Object and General Principles of Dressage, para. 6)

Above: *This horse probably feels light in the hand to the rider, but in fact he has brought his nose behind the vertical in order to avoid the contact.*

Left: *A horse who is relaxed and moving without constraint will be able to reach out and accept the contact with the rider's hands.*

Right: *This young pony is making a nice shape for a novice.*

of her hindlimbs and engage her hindquarters, lift her back and lighten her forehand. Only when these things happen will she come into the 'outline' which will enable her to move in self-carriage.

'On the bit'

Some trainers have suggested that 'on the aids' would be a better term to use, and I think they are right because being

It is perhaps a pity that the FEI used the term 'submissiveness' because this suggests that domination of the horse is somehow involved. As used here, however, all it means is that the horse is not showing any resistance to the

aids – which is reiterated in the last sentence. So being 'on the bit' has nothing to do with imposing a head carriage on the horse (which as we have seen is counterproductive): the horse comes to the bit, not the other way round.

At the start of serious training the horse may try to lean on the bit, using it as a kind of 'fifth leg'. Although she needs some support from the bit at this stage (as her neck muscles will still be comparatively undeveloped), she should not be encouraged to lean on the bit; if she starts to feel heavy in your hands, send her forwards more briskly. Bear in mind, though, that this leaning on the bit may be a sign

of fatigue, so do not tire her still further, but end the session, as always, on a good note. As the horse becomes stronger she will gradually start to lighten the contact, as she no longer needs to seek as much support from the rider's hands.

Above: A horse is said to be on the bit when the neck is more or less raised and arched according to the stage of training and the extension or collection of the pace, accepting the bridle with a light and soft contact and submissiveness throughout.

Work on a circle

This work is often decried as 'endless trotting in circles', yet correct work on circles is essential if the horse is to be made supple and free from crookedness.

How it benefits the horse

- When a horse is moving correctly on a circle her body must be bent throughout its length. As the inside of her body contracts, the outside stretches. The outside hind leg therefore has further to travel, while the inside hind leg must flex in order to step under the horse's body. The circle therefore plays a role both in suppling the horse and encouraging her to engage her hindquarters.
- If the work is correctly carried out on both reins, it will develop the muscles evenly on both sides, and the horse will find it easier to move straight.

The aids for riding a circle

Riders must beware of the temptation to ride a circle as if they were steering a bicycle. Too often we see horses 'jack-knifing' on a circle because riders have oversteered with their hands; the horse's neck is bent to the inside, but her body remains straight. This is of no value and may even be detrimental to the horse, as the neck muscles on the inside lock up and the back muscles stiffen. So care must be taken to ride circles correctly at all times.

The rider makes a small shift of his or her weight in the direction of the movement, as described in chapter 3, when we talked about the rider's seat. The inside leg touches the horse just behind the girth; this, as we have already established, will create the necessary flexion on that side. The rider's outside leg is positioned slightly further back to stop the hindquarters from swinging out and straightening the horse's body. The rider's shoulders must be parallel with the horse's shoulders; this means that the outer shoulder is slightly ahead of the inside shoulder. Some trainers disagree with this, saying that the rider's outside shoulder should not come forwards (and some even advocate that it should be slightly back). They reason that to bring the outside shoulder forwards puts a twist in the rider's body (see illustrations, right) and that this is detrimental to the rider.

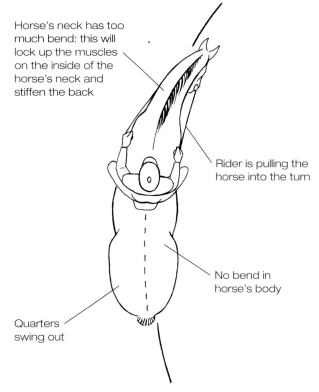

Horse's neck has too much bend: this will lock up the muscles on the inside of the horse's neck and stiffen the back

Rider is pulling the horse into the turn

No bend in horse's body

Quarters swing out

Above: Horse and rider 'jackknifing' on a circle.

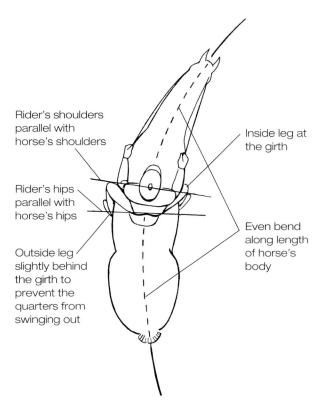

Rider's shoulders parallel with horse's shoulders

Inside leg at the girth

Rider's hips parallel with horse's hips

Even bend along length of horse's body

Outside leg slightly behind the girth to prevent the quarters from swinging out

Above: Riding a circle correctly.

This kind of 'twist' is exactly what back therapists advocate, however, as an exercise for people with certain back problems. Furthermore, if the rider's outside shoulder does not come forwards, then the outer hand must be brought forwards to allow for the bend in the horse's neck on that side, or the horse's neck will simply straighten as the rein does not give to allow for the bend. This means that the upper arm becomes weighted, making the contact on that side heavy. On the other hand, if the outer shoulder comes forwards, then the rider's hand automatically advances because the shoulder does; it does not give away the contact, but simply allows for the bend in the horse's neck.

Above left: The rider prepares to start the circle by looking in the direction she intends to ride the horse.

Left: Horse and rider start the turn into the circle.

Top: The horse is starting to bend round the rider's leg and step under his body with his inside hind leg.

Above: Returning to the track, this horse is leaning into the circle slightly. This is very common, as horses tend to resist the centrifugal force by putting weight on the inside shoulder. This tendency will gradually disappear as the horse becomes better balanced on the circle.

At the same time the rider must not collapse at the waist or bring the inside shoulder back; othewise, as with oversteering, the horse will simply 'jack-knife'. So riding a simple circle is not as straightforward as it first appears.

Be careful not to ask for too small a circle to begin with; if a horse cannot bend correctly on a large circle she will certainly not be able to do so on a smaller one. Start with circles of 20 m (66 ft) in diameter to begin with; once the horse is bending throughout her length on a circle of this size, you can progress to 10 m (33 ft) circles. If at any time it feels as if the horse is struggling on a smaller circle, go back to larger ones until she is once more comfortable with these, and only then attempt the smaller diameter circles again. Otherwise you will risk exposing your horse to strain and possible injury. The smallest diameter of circle demanded in a dressage test is 8 m (26 ft), so if you and your horse can manage a circle this small while maintaining a correct bend, you are doing rather well.

Top far left: This horse is well-balanced enough to be able to tackle a small circle.

Top left: Smaller circles demand a greater degree of bend throughout the horse's body.

Left: The horse is able to maintain impulsion throughout the circle.

Above: Without being in any way restrictive, the outside rein helps to prevent the horse from 'drifting out' through the turn.

If you find that your circles are irregularly shaped and you have difficulty 'seeing' the shape, think of containing the circle within a square, using markers to indicate the corners (this is obviously much easier if you are riding in an enclosed school). Start at one of the markers and ride a quarter of the circle to the next one, and so on. With practice you will find your circles become more regular.

Once the horse is happy working in smaller circles, you can ride lots of small circles all over the schooling area. Try riding one in each corner, first of all in walk, then in trot.

Work on circles should always be interspersed with work on straight lines. When you have completed each circle exercise, spend a few minutes riding forwards in a straight line, changing direction frequently to prevent the horse becoming stale.

Figure of eight

As the name suggests, the figure of eight is really just a couple of circles joined with a few strides in a straight line. When first starting to ride figures of eight, do not be

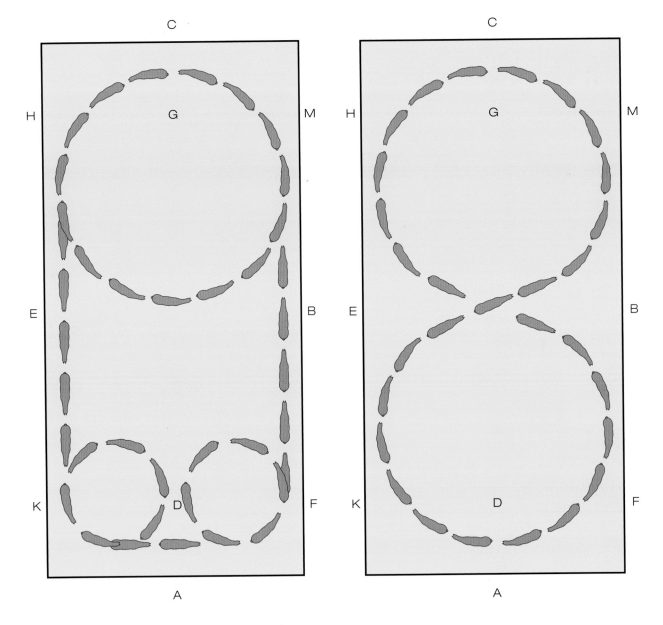

Above: *Circle exercises.*

Above: *Figure of eight.*

tempted to make the change of rein too abrupt. The horse needs time to adjust the bend of her body to the new direction, so allow her at least three strides to accomplish this (and don't forget to change your own position accordingly). This is especially important if the horse is quite stiff, as too sudden a change will cause her to lose rhythm and impulsion, which at this stage are more important than accuracy. Once she starts to bend more easily, you will find that you can ride the figures more precisely.

Below left: *Figure of eight: the rider starts with a 20 m (66 ft) circle on the left rein.*

Bottom left: *Riding the horse straight for several strides, the rider prepares to change the rein.*

Below: *Having changed the rein, the figure of eight will be completed by a 20 m (66 ft) circle right. The horse needs to bend slightly more on this rein than he is doing here.*

To begin with, ride a simple figure of eight formed by two 20 m (66 ft) circles, changing the rein at X. Once the horse is able to adjust the bend of her body through the change of rein in both walk and trot, progress to smaller figures of eight made up of two 10 m (33 ft) circles.

Loops

These are rather misleadingly named, as most of us think of a loop as something that turns back on itself. In the schooling arena, however, a loop means something different: the horse is initially ridden in a straight line along

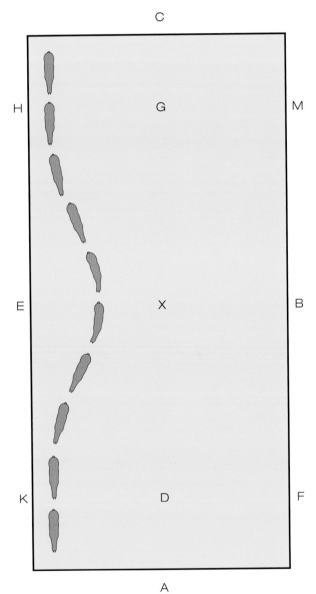

Above: Loop along the long side of the school.

the track, then brought in slightly off the track and ridden in a curve for a few strides, then brought back onto the track to continue in a straight line. It is one of the simplest exercises designed to promote bending.

Top left: *To ride a loop along the long side of the school, the rider brings the horse in off the track.*

Top right: *The horse is ridden in a curve for a few strides...*

Above: *...and then returns to the track.*

Serpentine

This is an extremely valuable exercise for both horse and rider, as it tests the rider's ability to give clear and precise aids, while at the same time asking the horse to change direction and bend several times within a comparatively short space of time.

maximize the benefit to the horse (and yourself). As with the figure of eight, allow the horse sufficient time to change her bend.

Below: *The rider starts a serpentine on the left rein...*

Bottom: *...and rides straight across the school to commence the next loop of the serpentine.*

Above: *Serpentine.*

It is usual practice to start a serpentine in the middle of one of the short sides of the school. In practice, however, you can ride one anywhere you like, as long as you take care to ride the curves as correctly as you can so as to

Demi-volte in walk and trot

The demi-volte is often referred to as a loop, which increases the confusion about what a loop is. A volte is simply a small circle; a demi-volte is a half-circle, ridden off the track and returning to the track on a diagonal line (see below). It is best to start riding demi-voltes in walk. Ride along the track until you come to a marker; half-halt and start a 10 m (33 ft) circle. Instead of completing the circle and returning to the track at the point from which you started, take a diagonal line which will bring you back to the

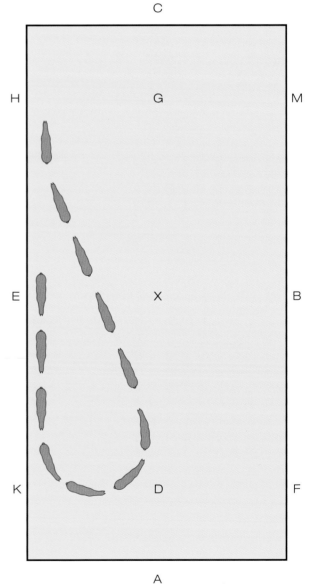

Top: Looking in the new direction, she changes her aids to help the horse to bend to the right...

Above: ...and rides straight across the school again.

Above: Demi-volte (loop).

track some distance behind the point at which you left it. Ride a series of demi-voltes in different places in the school, changing the direction as often as you can.

Once you can ride accurate demi-voltes in walk, try the exercise in trot.

Spiralling in and out

Spiralling in and out on circles is an excellent exercise which can be carried out in either trot or canter. It is especially useful for horses who tend to rush in either of these gaits. Start by riding a 20 m (66 ft) circle, gradually

Below: From a 20 m (66 ft) circle, gradually spiral in until the horse is making the smallest circle of which he is capable...

Bottom: ...then spiral out again. This horse is leaning in on the circle; spiralling in and out will help to counteract this as the exercise will help him to become more balanced.

Top: To ride the type of loop often referred to as a demi-volte, start with a half-circle.

Above left: The half-circle is ridden exactly as if it were a full circle...

Above right: ...but instead of completing the circle, the horse returns to the track in a straight line.

Above: Already the horse is bending more throughout his body and the trot has become more rhythmical.

spiralling in until the horse is making the smallest circle of which he is capable. Don't just pull the horse's head into the circle; step down into the inside stirrup slightly, and nudge the horse over gently with your outside thigh and knee. Spiral out again and finish with another 20 m (66 ft) circle. As always, repeat on both reins.

Small circles and lengthening across the diagonal

Provided the horse is able to bend properly on small circles, you can try this exercise. Ride the smallest circle you can, on the inside track in one corner of the school, maintaining the rhythm and forward momentum. As you come back to the inside track, ride across the diagonal and ask for more impulsion (remember the light touches with the leg). If the horse has completed the circle properly, you should find

that she lengthens her stride a little coming across the diagonal; this is rather like coiling up all the energy in the circle, then releasing it across the diagonal.

Top: From a small circle in trot...

Above: ...you can ask the horse for a few lengthened strides across the school.

Galloping as an exercise

Finally, this is an exercise that will not only aid relaxation and promote impulsion, but also begin to strengthen the horse's muscles.

Most horses in good health love to gallop, and riders in general find it exhilarating and enjoyable. The good news is that it is an excellent way of encouraging free, forward movement, freeing the horse's back and developing the muscles of the chest, shoulders and upper forelegs.

There are several points to remember when going for a gallop with a view to exercising the horse rather than just having a good time (you can do both at the same time):

- Choose your ground carefully. Horses can generally gallop over uneven ground much more easily than they can walk, trot or even canter over it because the feet are not in contact with the ground long enough for the horse to stumble too much. Even so, if the ground is very rutted or uneven, a horse can trip and take a nasty fall (as can her rider), so avoid galloping over such ground. Also avoid very hard ground as this will jar the horse's forelegs and may result in injury. Try to find a reasonably level area; if you know a sympathetic racehorse trainer with all-weather gallops, you may be able to cajole them into letting you use their gallops, or you might be able to hire them. Beaches can be a good place for a gallop if the sand is not too deep and soft; just near the shoreline sand may be firmer and many horses love a run along the beach. In some countries/areas you may need permission to ride on a beach, or there may be other restrictions, so always check beforehand

- Do not always gallop in the same place or the horse will start to anticipate it and may get too excited. Try to vary the place and timing, and do not gallop every time you go out to that particular area. Avoid galloping in company, too, as this will inevitably result in overexcitement, which you really want to avoid.

- Start off with gallops of short duration; if you feel the horse start to get too excited, bring her back down to a trot, then a walk, until she has calmed down again and before things get out of hand. Gradually extend the periods of work at the gallop until the horse will gallop steadily for prolonged periods without getting excited; as long as they are asked to gallop regularly rather than only occasionally, most horses soon learn that this is work and not an occasion for high jinks. Although racehorses do sometimes get excited when training at the gallop, most of them settle quite readily to this work, as they are accustomed to it.

- Do not overtax a horse who is unfit; short periods of galloping will not harm her (after all, horses gallop freely in the fields), but you will need to work up gradually to regular spells of galloping. If necessary, seek the advice of a veterinary surgeon.

By interspersing work in the school with periods of fast work outside the school, you will encourage the free, forward movement that will help your horse to perform like the great athlete she truly is.

Top: Galloping is an excellent way of encouraging free, forward movement, freeing the horse's back and developing the muscles of the chest, shoulders and upper forelegs.

CHAPTER 8

Improving suppleness and muscle strength

IN THIS chapter we look at exercises designed to improve the horse's suppleness and muscle strength, to continue to promote engagement of the hindquarters and introduce the horse to the beginnings of collection.

Deep work

In the last two decades of the twentieth century a number of dressage trainers and riders started to make use of a training technique, often referred to by its German name, *rollkür*, which involved extreme flexion of the horse's neck. This technique was widely copied, often by riders who did not understand what it was intended to do. It began to be widely criticized by many very eminent riders and trainers, including the late Dr Reiner Klimke, and there is still a great deal of controversy surrounding its use. I mention it here because some readers may have come across this controversy and been put off the idea of deep work as a result. I want to make it clear that the deep work being described here is not the same as *rollkür*; it has been around for much longer and is recognized as being beneficial by classical trainers all over the world. In order to reap that benefit, however, as with all exercises, you must carry it out correctly. This is especially the case with deep work because, along with its benefits, it brings certain risks that have to be taken seriously. So what is it, what does it entail and how does it benefit the horse?

Deep work involves working the horse with his head and neck lowered, his topline rounded and his hindquarters engaged. It can be carried out on the lunge (often in conjunction with a training aid such as the Chambon or de Gogue) or under saddle. It is often confused with 'long and low', but the latter does not necessarily involve rounding of the topline and is mainly used for relaxation, whereas true deep work really makes the horse's muscles work. Its benefits are:

- When the horse lowers his head and engages his hindquarters, traction is exerted on the nuchal ligament, which helps to raise the horse's back.
- Engagement of the hindquarters involves flexion of the lumbo-sacral joint, which helps to strengthen and develop the muscles of the hindquarters and mobilizes the hip joint.
- The back is suppled because the vertebral column has to stretch longitudinally.
- The muscles of the abdomen have to work harder, which strengthens them and improves their ability to assist the topline in supporting the spine.
- The muscles at the base of the neck are developed and strengthened.
- The pectoral muscles have to work harder, strengthening them and improving their ability to assist in supporting the forehand.

Still, this work does have its drawbacks. If the work is carried out with the horse's topline overstretched, this can result in damage to the supraspinous ligament and even to the spine itself. On the other hand, if the horse's hindquarters are not engaged, the topline will not be stretched and the horse will simply fall onto his forehand, increasing stress on the already vulnerable forelimbs. This is why deep work is best introduced on the lunge, while the horse is free from the weight of a rider and where hindquarters can be observed to ensure they are active enough. Whether on the lunge or under saddle, this work must not be carried out too frequently or prolonged for more than about ten minutes on each rein (it would be best to work up to this gradually).

Right: Deep work involves working the horse with his head and neck lowered, his topline rounded and his hindquarters engaged.

Deep work should never be started until the horse is relaxed, warmed up and has started to engage his hindquarters. With the horse going forwards in an active trot, ask him to lower his head in the manner described on page 94 under 'Long and low'. As with that exercise, the horse's head should never be forcibly lowered or pulled in, or the whole point of the exercise will be lost. You can help the horse by easing your weight slightly more onto your thighs, *without* bringing your seat off the saddle. If the horse is going forwards with impulsion and is really using his back and hindquarters, you will be able to feel his back rounding underneath you.

Shoulder-in

In the shoulder-in the horse's forehand is brought in slightly to the inside so that the path followed by the hind and forefeet forms three tracks. The outside hind foot forms the outside track, the inside hind and outside forefeet form the middle track, and the inside forefoot forms the inside track. The inside foreleg crosses over the outside foreleg, and the inside hind leg crosses in front of the outside hind leg. The horse's body must be bent throughout its whole length and not just through the neck, or the result will be a simple leg yield rather than a shoulder-in, and the exercise will cease to be beneficial.

How the shoulder-in benefits the horse

- The inside hind leg has to flex more in order to step under the horse's body. This engages the hindquarters and enables the horse to take more weight on the hind legs.
- This increased flexion means that the inside hock is strengthened.
- The long muscles of the horse's body on the inside are contracted, while the long muscles on the outside are correspondingly stretched.
- The back is raised and rounded.
- The inside foreleg crosses in front of the outside fore, freeing and suppling the shoulders, which helps to straighten the horse.
- Increased engagement of the hindquarters allows greater freedom of movement of the forehand.

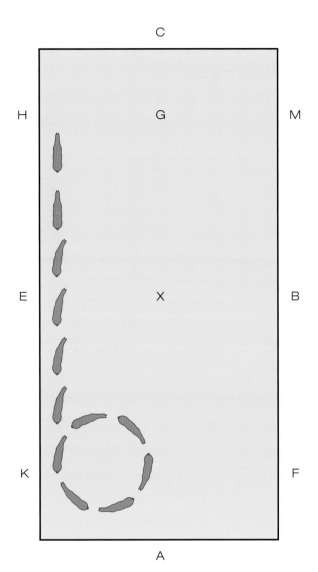

Above: Shoulder-in exercise.

In order to be of any benefit, the shoulder-in must be ridden correctly. If it is performed incorrectly, at best it has no value and at worst it can actually be damaging. Unfortunately, some horse-training books show examples of a shoulder-in with the horse not bending his body at all or flexing his hocks and, worst of all, with his neck very much overflexed. This can 'disconnect' and eventually weaken the muscles at the base of the neck, which as we have seen are essential for the horse to be able to carry himself correctly.

The aids for shoulder-in

Ride the horse as if you were about to commence a circle, but as his shoulders start to come off the track, make a half-

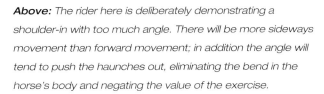

Above: The rider here is deliberately demonstrating a shoulder-in with too much angle. There will be more sideways movement than forward movement; in addition the angle will tend to push the haunches out, eliminating the bend in the horse's body and negating the value of the exercise.

Top left: Here the rider is demonstrating what happens when all the bend is in the horse's neck; the horse's body remains straight, and the exercise becomes pointless.

Top right: In a correct shoulder-in the horse's forehand is brought in slightly to the inside so that the path followed by the hind and forefeet forms three tracks.

Above left: The rider keeps her shoulders and hips parallel with the horse's shoulders and hips.

Above right: The rider's outside leg behind the girth helps to prevent the horse's quarters from falling out.

halt and continue up the track. The inside leg just at or fractionally behind the girth encourages the horse to move both forwards and sideways with small, electric touches; the outside leg remains passive behind the girth to prevent the quarters from swinging out and straightening the horse's

body. Stepping lightly into the outside stirrup will cause a slight shift of your weight to the outside, which will also encourage the horse to move sideways as he will want to step under your weight. The rider's hips and shoulders remain parallel to the horse's hips and shoulders, and as always you should look between the horse's ears; the position of your head will help to keep the horse's forehand in slightly off the track. Of course you will want to see where you are going up the track, so it is permissible to glance sideways without moving your head.

Shoulder-in exercises

The simplest shoulder-in exercise consists of riding the horse in shoulder-in along the long side of the arena or schooling area. If you are not using a conventional arena, you can still adapt this exercise to other conditions, provided you have a reasonably straight line to follow (such as a hedge, wall, fence, line on the ground, etc.). This and more complex exercises should initially be ridden in walk, as the horse will find it easier to begin with and you will have more time to correct your position if things get a little disorganized. Once the shoulder-in at a walk is established, progress to riding the exercise at the trot (go rising so as to free the horse's back). This will give the exercise more impulsion and it will therefore be of greater gymnastic benefit.

Start by riding the smallest circle your horse can comfortably manage, in one corner of the school. As you return to the track, carry on up the long side in shoulder-in. Be satisfied with one or two steps of shoulder-in to begin with; one step executed correctly is worth more than six or seven incorrect steps.

When the horse is able to maintain the shoulder-in correctly for at least five or six strides, you can start to vary the place and timing of the exercises. You can try riding across the school in shoulder-in, up the centre line or along the quarter-lines (see the arena layouts shown on page 18). You can even try some steps of shoulder-in when riding out; in fact, it has some added benefits. Suppose you are riding along a road or a trail, and your horse is reluctant to pass something at the side of the road or path. If you ask him for shoulder-in you will very often find that he will pass the offending object without fuss because he is slightly turned away from it and is further distracted from it by being asked to do something other than ride straight forwards. I have used shoulder-in to get spooky horses past manhole covers on the road, killer trees, tractors, monsters lurking in postboxes and even, in the case of a horse with a phobia about black-and-white animals, a herd of Friesian cows.

Above left: *The horse's inside foreleg crosses over the outside foreleg.*

Above right: *Watching the shoulder-in from the rear, we can see quite clearly the bend in the horse's body.*

Far left: *This horse is able to maintain the shoulder-in along the long side of the school. More novice horses may only be able to produce a few good steps of shoulder-in at first.*

Left: *Here we can see the inside hind limb flexing as it comes forward under the horse's body.*

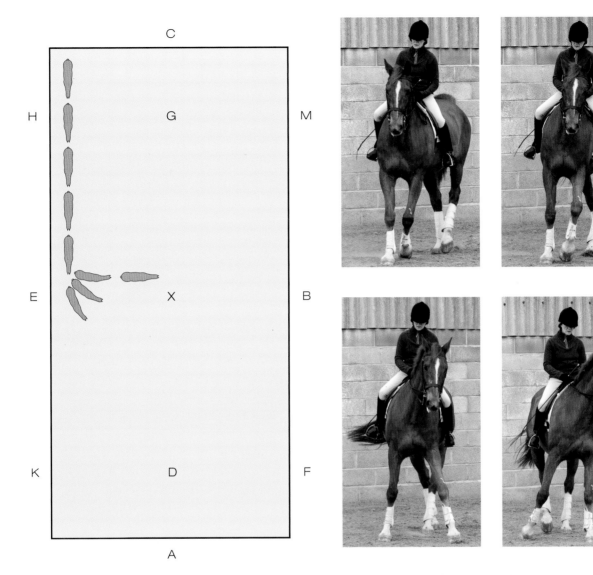

Above: Turn on the haunches.

Turn on the haunches

The turn on the haunches is sometimes also referred to as a 'quarter turn'. So what is it? In walk, the horse makes a 90-degree turn by moving his outside hind foot and his two forefeet around the inside hind leg, which does not remain stationary, but takes very small steps in place.

How the turn on the haunches benefits the horse

As with all exercises that require the horse to bend his body and step further under his body, the turn on the haunches helps to make him more supple and encourages him to flex his hind legs and engage the hindquarters.

Top left: Turn on the haunches: the horse makes a 90-degree turn by moving his outside hind foot and his two forefeet around the inside hind leg.

Top right: The horse does not simply pivot on the inside hind foot; the latter does not remain stationary but takes very small steps in place.

Above left: The horse must bend his trunk and step further under his body.

Above right: The footfall sequence of the walk is maintained.

The aids for the turn on the haunches

As for the shoulder-in, start by riding a small circle. Decide beforehand where you want to make the turn, and ride your circle so that you return to the track just before that point. Keeping the horse slightly flexed to the inside, ride forwards for a couple of steps. Half-halt as you invite the horse into the turn by touching his side lightly with your inside lower leg and moving your inside seatbone forwards slightly, at the same time stepping down into the stirrup and rotating your inside hand outwards just a fraction. The outside rein should lie passively against the horse's neck, while your outside leg just behind the girth prevents the horse's quarters from swinging round. The outside thigh and knee can assist by nudging the horse round into the

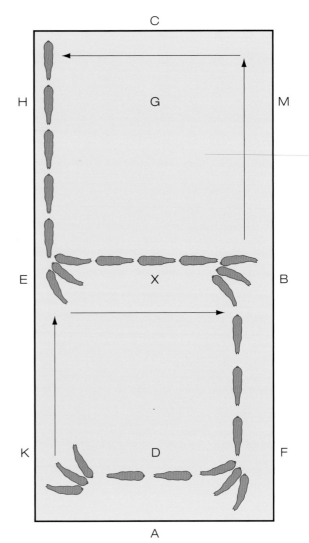

Above: *Turn on the haunches: exercise 2.*

turn. When he has completed the turn you should immediately ride straight forwards.

Eventually the horse should be able to accomplish the turn within two or three steps, but to begin with you may need to allow him to take more steps than this. Although the horse is moving sideways more than forwards, you should still think in terms of riding forwards and not allow the horse to grind to a halt.

Exercise 1

Ride around the perimeter of your schooling area in walk. Just before you arrive at each corner, instead of riding into the corner make a quarter turn across the school; repeat this at each corner. (You can ride the same exercise using only half the school.)

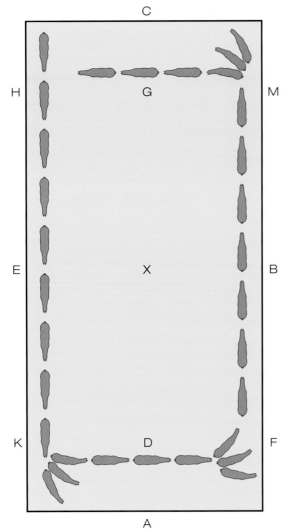

Above: *Turn on the haunches: exercise 1.*

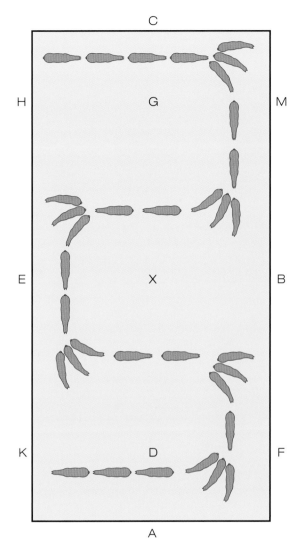

Above: Turn on the haunches: exercise 3

These exercises are quite demanding, so do not attempt them until the horse can make the turns correctly. As always, if the horse seems to be having difficult in complying, do not persist, but instead go back to something simpler.

Demi-pirouette

Like the turn on the haunches, the demi-pirouette is ridden in walk (it can of course be ridden in canter as a preliminary to the canter pirouette, but as this is an advanced movement we will concern ourselves only with the demi-pirouette in walk).

The aids are the same as for the turn on the haunches, except that, instead of simply making a quarter turn, the movement is continued until the horse is facing in the

Exercise 2

Ride along one side of the school, making a quarter turn left at E; ride across the school and make a quarter turn right at B; continue through F and make another quarter turn right at the corner. Make a third quarter turn right in the next corner and a fourth quarter turn right at E. Ride across the school and make a quarter turn left at B. Carry on round the school, repeating the turns on the left rein until you come back to E.

Exercise 3

Ride a serpentine in walk, making a quarter turn every time you change direction.

Above: Demi-pirouette.

Far left: The demi-pirouette is effectively a continuation of the turn on the haunches.

Left: The horse bends around the rider's inside leg.

Below left: This is a creditable first effort on the part of a novice horse.

Bottom left: Although after his first attempt he is still on the forehand, this work will benefit this horse enormously as it will help him to engage his hindquarters and take more weight behind.

opposite direction from the one he started out in. The easiest way to ride a demi-pirouette is along the long side of the school (although it can of course be ridden anywhere). As with the turn on the haunches, the footfall sequence of the walk must be maintained (in other words, the horse must still pick up all his feet and not just pivot around a fixed inside hind foot), as well as the forward movement.

Rein back

The rein back is a very good exercise for getting the horse to engage his hindquarters, but as with all such exercises it must be done correctly or it will be of no benefit, and executed poorly it can actually be harmful.

Left: Preparing for the rein-back, the rider asks for a half-halt in walk.

Top: As he starts to step backwards, the horse moves his legs in diagonal pairs.

Above: The rider uses her leg behind the girth to maintain the backward movement, but she does not pull back with the reins.

Top right: The horse halts, but is ready to move off again immediately.

The movement is badly named as it implies that the rider pulls on the rein to make the horse go back; unfortunately this is all too often exactly what happens. In a correct rein back, the horse moves his legs diagonally in pairs as in trot, rather than in the four-beat sequence of the walk. The horse has to take weight back onto his hocks; his back is braced and he lifts his withers and the base of his neck. When it is incorrect – usually because the rider is pulling on the reins – the horse raises his head and neck, his back hollows and he has to shuffle backwards because there is no support for his back. This can result in strain injuries to the neck, shoulders and back.

The aids for rein back are:

- Bring the horse to a halt, as square as you can get it.
- Ease your seat slightly more onto your thighs; this will help to free the horse's back.
- With your legs lightly against the horse's sides slightly behind the girth, give the leg aids for walk on.
- At the same time, resist slightly with the hands; there must be no backward movement – just a closing of the fingers on the reins.
- When the horse steps back, immediately ask for forward movement again.

To begin with, ask for only a couple of steps back, and be content if the horse gives you just the one correct step back.

123

If it all falls to pieces, do not worry. Simply ride forwards again, come to a halt and try again.

It takes some horses a little while to grasp what is wanted, and some may move their hindquarters to one side until they gain better control of their hind legs while moving backwards. It may help certain horses if a helper on the ground puts a little pressure on the horse's chest to encourage him to move back, but if the rein back is correctly ridden most horses will soon get the idea.

Raised trotting poles and cavalletti

In chapter 6 we saw how beneficial working over trotting poles can be. We can take this work a stage further by raising the poles off the ground.

Left, bottom left and above: Work over raised poles aids the development of the horse's muscles and encourages engagement of the hindquarters.

This aids the development of the horse's muscles and encourages engagement of the hindquarters because:

- the horse has to lift his feet over the raised poles, and therefore has to flex the lumbo-sacral joint as well as the hocks and stifle;
- this exercises the muscles of the abdomen and back as well as the hindquarters;
- increased flexion of the hind limbs helps to build more elevation into the gaits;
- the amount of effort involved meant that this work improves general fitness and stamina.

Ordinary trotting poles can be raised by supporting them on virtually anything as long as it is the right height and is stable enough to prevent it from being overturned if a pole is knocked. The working height of raised poles is generally around 15–20 cm (6–8 in), but of course you can vary this to suit the individual horse.

In Europe, work over raised poles is often carried out using poles set (or fixed in place) on crosspieces. As the crosspieces are not symmetrical, they can be turned over to vary the height, which makes them more versatile than poles simply raised on whatever support is available. Raised poles constructed in this manner are known as *cavalletti*.

Jumping (gridwork)

People tend not to associate jumping with schooling on the flat, yet at one time, when dressage as a sport was in its infancy, all dressage tests included a small jump. Tackling low jumps in a systematic way can be very beneficial in encouraging horses to round their backs and get their hocks underneath them; it carries on the work started over raised poles.

Above right: Grid work: trotting poles will help the horse to get into the correct rhythm for the fence.

Right: The rider folds at the hip-joints instead of remaining upright; this helps to free the horse's back.

Below: Tackling low jumps in a systematic way can be very beneficial in encouraging horses to round their backs and get their hocks underneath them.

Exercise 1

Set out a row of three or four trotting poles 1.2–1.7 m (4–5.3 in) apart. About 2–2.75 m (6.5–9 ft) after the last pole, set up a small cross-pole. The trotting poles will help the horse to get into the correct rhythm for the fence, provided the rider does not interfere. Do not be tempted to throw yourself up the horse's neck as so many riders do when tackling even small fences; the correct jumping position is simply the classical position with the stirrups shortened (by how much will depend on the individual rider). The rider folds at the hip joints instead of remaining upright; this helps to free the horse's back.

Exercise 2

As for exercise 2, except that after the crosspole there is a parallel jump set about 4.5–5.5 m (15–18 ft) beyond it. The rider must remain as still as possible between the jumps so as not to unbalance the horse.

Exercise 3

Set out two cross-poles about 3–3.7m (10–12 ft) apart, with a trotting pole about 1.9–2.75 m (6–9 ft) in front of the first cross-pole.

As with ordinary trotting poles, you may need to adjust the distances slightly to suit the individual horse. Once the horse is tackling the above exercises with confidence, raise the height of the poles slightly, but do not ask too much, too soon. These are gymnastic exercises that the horse must carry out with confidence and in balance and rhythm. Otherwise their value is lost.

Riding up and down hills

If you are fortunate enough to live in an area with hilly terrain nearby, take advantage of it. Riding up and down hills is a marvellous way to strengthen and supple your horse while enjoying the scenery. In order to negotiate a steep slope efficiently, a horse must lower his head and neck, and flex the joints of his hindquarters and hocks. This applies whether he is going up or coming down again. Riding uphill you can start in walk, gradually progressing to trot and canter as the horse gains in strength. Coming down again, however, you should stay in walk, especially if the slope is steep, as a horse coming downhill at speed will gather momentum and may lose his balance. For this work

to be of any benefit, the horse needs to be balanced and using his hindquarters properly, which he may not do if he is scrambling down the hill. Many riders lean back when coming down hills, hampering the horse's ability to use his back muscles and hindquarters. Whether riding up or down hills, ease your weight slightly off the horse's back and more onto your thighs, to enable him to round up and get his hocks underneath him.

What can you do if you live in a completely flat area? Depending on your circumstances, you may be able to construct an artificial mound somewhere in a field. This might be on the expensive side if it involves digging up earth and resiting it. If you board your horse out (and the livery owner gives permission for such a construction), you might be able to share the cost (and the use of the artificial

'hill') with other people boarding their horses there. The mound does not have to be too high to be of benefit. At my yard there is such a mound in the grass *manège*; it is slightly less than 2 m (6.5 ft) high, and over the years it has proved invaluable, especially in the training of youngstock.

All the above exercises, if carried out correctly, will enhance your horse's muscular strength and suppleness. With increased engagement of the hindquarters will come a lightening of the forehand; as the horse starts to collect himself more, he will become more athletic and responsive,

and – if he is judiciously rewarded for good work – will come to enjoy and hopefully even look forward to his work.

Opposite: *In order to negotiate a slope efficiently, a horse must lower his head and neck and flex the joints of his hindquarters and hocks.*

Above: *Whether riding up or down hills, ease your weight slightly off the horse's back and more onto your thighs, to enable him to round up and get his hocks underneath him.*

127

Adapting and tailoring exercises

NO MATTER how much they may differ in size and appearance, all horses belong to the same species and have the same skeletal structure. This means that the principles of training apply to all horses, regardless of breed or type. Differences between breeds and types, however, mean that we have to tailor the ways in which we apply those principles in order to take account of those differences. If we recognize that such differences exist, and

that certain types or individuals need a different approach from others, we know that we have to be flexible in how we think about training them.

There are around 300 recognized breeds and types of horse and pony today, but there is not nearly as much variation between them as there is among the many breeds of dog. If we consider the ways in which some of the main breeds and types need different approaches to training, we can easily adapt that knowledge to other breeds and types which may be similar in many ways.

The horse world has generally divided breeds into three separate categories: hotbloods, warmbloods and coldbloods. These terms do not refer to the actual blood temperature, of course; equine body temperature is normally in the region of 37.5°C to 38.6°C (101.5–99.5°F) regardless of breed. The terms refer instead to the perceived characteristics of a breed. So Arabians, generally thought of as being fiery and reactive, are considered to be hotbloods. The various warmbloods, as their name suggests, are usually thought of as calmer in temperament and less sensitive, while the various draught horses are often viewed as rather phlegmatic, possibly sluggish and not very responsive.

The hotbloods (which include, of course, the Thoroughbred as well as the Arabian) are often thought of as being the foundation for all other breeds of riding horse. This is a gross oversimplification; most of our modern breeds have all kinds of different breeds and types in their ancestry. Many people also consider the Iberian breeds (the Purebred Spanish horse, or Andalusian, and its cousin the Lusitano) to be hotbloods that have also contributed a great deal to modern breeds, and both historical and equine genetic research is suggesting that this is indeed the case.

Left: The Arabian is generally regarded as a hotblood. This Arabian stallion is called Rabanat.

When is a horse physically mature?

We are often told that certain breeds, such as the Throughbred, are early maturing and that in the case of Thoroughbreds this is what makes it possible to start their racing careers so early. This is not the case. Dr Deb Bennett, who as a palaeontologist knows about rates of skeletal growth and maturity, has this to say: 'No horse, at any time, anywhere, has ever been physically mature before the age of five and a half.' (*Conquerors: The Roots of New World Horsemanship*, 1998.) This is the earliest age at which

Left: *The Irish Draught is derived from both hot-blooded and cold-blooded stock.*

Below: *Together with the Arabian and the Iberian breeds, the Thoroughbred has contributed a great deal to many of our modern horse breeds.*

the cartilaginous growth plates that occur throughout the horse's entire skeleton finish closing. Those of the spine are the last to close, and in some horses, especially bigger ones, this closure may not take place until the horse is seven or eight. Asking the horse to perform hard work before her skeleton has fully matured risks damaging her permanently.

The masters of equitation of earlier times understood this perfectly well, which is why they warned against asking too much, too soon. Nowadays we are in such a rush in every aspect of our lives that this consideration for the horse seems to have fallen by the wayside. So often riders are encouraged to believe that they must achieve this or that with their horse before she is X years old, or otherwise they have somehow failed some test of competence or

commitment to some unspoken ideal. This is also nonsense and we should resist it strongly, for the horse's sake.

The Arabian

Arabian horses have been prized throughout much of equestrian history, not only for their beauty and elegance, but also for their affectionate temperaments, trainability and sensitivity.

One persistent belief about Arabians is that they have fewer thoracic and lumbar vertebrae than other breeds. It is

Below: Arabian horses have been prized throughout much of equestrian history, not only for their beauty and elegance but also for their affectionate temperaments, trainability and sensitivity.

true that some Arabians have only 17 thoracic vertebrae rather than the 18 (or even 19) possessed by most breeds, but many have the same number of vertebrae as most other types of horse. Arabians also generally have six lumbar vertebrae, just like most horses of other breeds. The Arabian's generally short back is determined by the length of the individual vertebrae, not by their number.

Arabians are sensitive horses who may react strongly to external stimuli, which means they often have a high muscle tone at rest. This high resting muscle tone generally goes with fast reflexes; the down side is that it may make the horse's back seem rather stiff, although Arabians are perfectly capable of bending once this stiffness is overcome. Such horses will need a training programme which emphasizes – to begin with, at least – exercises that promote relaxation and stretching. Suppling exercises may have to come before those which aid contact or impulsion, depending on the individual horse.

Another problem frequently encountered with Arabians is their tendency to hollow under saddle, poke their noses and stick their heads in the air. Many writers and trainers have even suggested that this is because Arabians are 'bred to go with their heads in the air'. This is just silly – a riding horse who habitually went with her head in the air would be potentially dangerous to her rider because not only would she be unable to see where she was going, but also it would be very difficult to control her. The raised head and hollow back in Arabians are caused by tension, which may be the result of excitement or apprehension, or it may be a response to pressure on the back: many Arabians are very sensitive in this respect and need tactful riding. The cure for this is the same as with any horse who raises her head and hollows her back: correct riding and the kind of training which encourages her to relax, round her back and become absorbed in her work.

The Thoroughbred

The emphasis on breeding for speed above all else means that Thoroughbreds can vary in appearance much more than is usually the case in breeds with a closed stud book. Some are quite angular and rangy, while others appear much chunkier and rounder. It is common, however, to find Thoroughbreds – and horses with a lot of Thoroughbred blood – who are rather long in the back and narrow in the chest. If length in the back is due to a long

Above: This Thoroughbred is quite long in the back but most of the length is in his ribcage. This makes him more flexible laterally than if the length were in his loins. The rider is opening the rein slightly to invite this novice horse into the turn.

ribcage, then, as long as the loin (the area between the last rib and the point of croup) is short, the back will be flexible enough laterally. If, however, the ribcage is short and the loin area long, this is a weak conformation which will predispose the horse to strain unless the rider is very correct in his or her position and is considerate of the horse's back. With such horses the emphasis will need to be on exercises which strengthen the back and abdomen (riding up and down slopes, deep work once the horse can begin to engage, work over raised poles, systematic gridwork), together with some basic lateral work to strengthen the forehand as well as the back (shoulder-in, turns on the haunches, demi-pirouettes in walk).

Warmbloods

People often talk about the 'warmblood' as if that described a single, easily identifiable breed. In fact there are many different breeds and types of warmblood, although almost all of them are notable for their power, athleticism and freedom of movement. They were originally bred in central Europe for cavalry purposes, by crossing native draught or carriage horses with Spanish horses, Arabians and Thoroughbreds. This produced horses with sufficient

strength to carry a cavalryman all day and over tough terrain, while retaining some of the speed and refinement of the lighter, hot-blooded breeds.

The modern sport horses collectively known as warmbloods are derived from these cavalry horses.

Right: *16.2 hh gelding by Maximillian Voltucky (KWPN – Dutch Warmblood) out of a part Trakehner mare.*

Below: *Warmbloods are often crossed with Thoroughbreds and Arabians to add fire and refinement. This gelding is by a Belgian Warmblood stallion out of a pure-bred Arabian mare.*

Left: Sweden has produced some magnificent Warmbloods, among them this horse, named Max, ridden by renowned dressage rider Kyra Kirklund.

Below: Along with many other European countries, Denmark has produced some superb Warmbloods.

Highly selective breeding based on proven performance has resulted in horses who are often considered to be the supreme equine athlete – an epithet once bestowed on the Thoroughbred. Warmbloods are bred all over the world, but are generally called after their place of origin. So we have the Hanoverian, from Saxony in Germany; the Trakehner from what used to be East Prussia; and Belgian and Dutch warmbloods, the latter derived from native breeds such as the Gelderlander, still prized for the sport of carriage-driving. Sweden also has its own warmblood, as do Poland, Bulgaria and numerous other European countries.

Many people fall into the trap of assuming that warmbloods require only minimal riding and training because these horses tend to have such impressive movement and obvious athleticism. Riders may also be misled by a warmblood's size and evident power into thinking that such horses are physically mature when in fact they are not. Warmbloods may actually be slow-maturing, not only physically, but also in some cases psychologically. People accustomed to the more reactive hotbloods sometimes refer to them as rather 'thick', but this is not really the case. Many warmbloods are simply more phlegmatic and 'laid-back' than the more reactive types, and may lack the sharpness of reaction to the aids that characterizes, say, Arabians or the Iberian breeds. For this reason it may be necessary to be more positive with the aids. For example, our home-bred warmblood gelding

needs a slightly more emphatic leg aid (by this I do not mean kicking, but a more brisk touch of the leg) than does our Arabian gelding or Arabian stallion, both of whom will respond to the lightest of touches. This does not mean that all warmbloods are lacking in sensitivity; much depends on how much Thoroughbred or Arabian blood they possess.

Warmbloods tend to have a fairly low resting muscle tone, which makes them less prone to the kind of back tension that can afflict more reactive breeds such as the Arabian. While their size and horizontal build makes it easy for them to produce big, extended gaits, this can result in some of them finding it more difficult to raise the forehand. What we see all too often in dressage tests, even at the highest level, is a false raising of the forehand, with the horse's back hollowed, his hocks disengaged and his withers sunk between his shoulder blades. Such horses may need to be ridden forwards briskly with the head and neck lowered until the muscles at the base of the neck are strong enough to raise the base of the neck.

Some warmbloods may also – perhaps because of their 'laid-back' nature – be rather 'backward-thinking'. These types will benefit from periods of controlled fast work to get them thinking more about forward movement.

The Iberians: the Lusitano and the Purebred Spanish horse

The Iberian breeds were originally bred for war; horses from the Iberian peninsula were much prized by the Romans, especially for their cavalry. Their agility, trainability and superb temperaments made them especially suited to stock work and to the mounted bullfight.

The Iberians tend to find collection easy because of their conformation; the short-coupled back, high-set neck and powerful chest and shoulders enable them to lower the quarters and push the neck and shoulders up with less effort than horses of many other breeds. They may sometimes, however, be rather stiff laterally because of the shortness of the back; such horses will need lots of suppling exercises such as shoulder-in, work on circles, etc.

Some people also find the Iberian breeds rather 'stuffy' because, with them, impulsion is directed not only forwards, but also upwards; it may also be because their

stride is shorter than that of more horizontally conformed horses such as Thoroughbreds and warmbloods. The croup is rather more sloping than in many breeds, which assists collection, but if too sloping can restrict the forward reach of the hind legs. Iberians can certainly move forwards at speed, however, and they can also extend beautifully; the result may simply not be as spectacular as it is with the bigger-moving warmbloods. Unfortunately, the fact that

Above: *Lusitano stallion Quem Foi, owned and ridden by Katharine Duckett.*

Opposite: *Sylvia Loch with her Lusitano stallion Prazer.*

Iberian horses can collect so easily means that they are sometimes ridden for too long in collection, which cramps their gaits. Even if this is not the case, all Iberians will benefit from being ridden freely outside the school; they should also frequently be ridden long and low to encourage them to stretch the topline.

These are noble horses whose sensitivity and responsiveness should be nurtured by equally sensitive riding.

North America has produced many fine breeds of horse, and it seems unfair to single only two out; however, the Quarter Horse is now one of the world's most popular breeds, as well as one of the most versatile, while the Saddlebred must surely be one of the most elegant.

The Quarter horse

This is a very powerful, compact horse whose speed, balance and agility have made it – alongside the Iberian breeds – the most effective stock horse in the world. Quarter horses are renowned for their ability to 'turn on a dime', as the saying goes, from a racing gallop. Indeed, it was as a racehorse that the Quarter horse earned its name – from its speed over a quarter of a mile (not, as many people think, from the size of the horse's quarters, immensely powerful though these are).

Quarter horses are chunky, muscular horses whose power and agility derives mainly from the massive hindquarters. With the revival of interest in Quarter horse racing near the end of the twentieth century, however, breeders started to introduce more Thoroughbred blood as an outcross. This has resulted in changes to the old Quarter horse type, with some representatives of the breed now appearing much less stocky and muscular. In such horses, as the quarters have become less powerful, some of the old agility has also been lost. There was a tendency for even some of the old type of Quarter horse to stand a little croup-high and for the shoulder to be somewhat loaded. These points of conformation did not matter so much because the hindquarters were powerful enough, and the

Below: Quarter horses are renowned for their power and agility and are now very popular all over the world.

Above: The American Saddlebred is a very elegant, well-conformed horse, with a lively yet co-operative nature.

flexion of the joints great enough, to offset a tendency for the forehand to be overloaded. If the hindquarters have lost some of their bulk and power, and the hindlimbs some of their ability to flex, then there is little to balance the overloaded forehand. Such horses will need lots of work over raised trotting poles or cavalletti, interspersed with gridwork, to strengthen the quarters and counterbalance the heavy forehand. Fortunately, there are still many of the old type of Quarter horses around.

The Saddlebred

Next to the Quarter horse, the breed that comes most readily to mind when one thinks of North American horses is probably the American Saddlebred. If we ignore the show-ring image of a high-stepping horse with heavily shod feet, nicked, high-set tail and pulled-in, false head carriage, we find a very elegant, well-conformed horse with a lively yet co-operative nature. The quarters may sometimes lack power and the pelvis may be a little too level; this tends to

set the hind legs too far back and makes it more difficult for the horse to engage the quarters, as the muscles which flex the lumbo-sacral joint and lower the quarters have a longer span and have to work harder to do the job. Exercises such as work over raised poles, gridwork, deep work, riding up and down slopes, etc. will help to strengthen the quarters and the abdominal muscles.

We can see from even these few examples that different types of horse may need a slightly different approach, depending on their physical type and personality. If we have sufficient understanding of the principles which underlie training, and of how these principles work with the horse's physical structure, we will be able to apply this understanding to the training of any horse, no matter what her breed or type.

Troubleshooting

TODAY THERE are many trainers who profess to use the horse's natural behaviour in solving problems. Some of these are very good, but all too often the tendency is to regard all problems as having a basis in behaviour. Explanations commonly put forward include: lack of respect for the rider/handler; rider/handler's failure to make the horse regard them as the 'herd leader'; the horse is 'trying it on' and so on. Although pain and fear are sometimes cited as possible causes, seldom are these properly addressed. Yet these are by far the commonest causes of problems, especially under saddle. Any attempt to solve problems of any kind must always begin by exploring

those two possibilities. Otherwise you may well make the horse suppress his problem behaviour, but you will not have addressed what is causing that behaviour in the first place.

Bucking

Bucking is often regarded as misbehaviour or even as a vice, yet it can occur for many reasons, most of them having nothing to do with deliberate misbehaviour on the part of the horse.

Below: Bucking can occur for many reasons. This horse simply lost his balance and bucked to try and regain it.

Possible causes

We are often told that the very act of riding a horse provokes a fear reaction in him, as he associates it with a predator jumping on his back, and that this is what causes a horse to buck. However, when horses buck or leap about when first backed, it is much more likely that they are reacting to the unbalancing effect of a weight on their backs.

Pain or irritation under the saddle is a common cause of bucking, as is loss of balance. If you watch horses cavorting about, especially on hilly or uneven ground, you will often see them lose their balance and give a buck to compensate. This is the equivalent of a human runner who trips and gives a skip in the air to regain his or her balance. Overfreshness and exuberance are other common causes.

Solution

If properly prepared for being ridden, habituated to the sensation of the saddle, and gradually accustomed to the feeling of weight on their backs, most horses do not react

violently to the presence of a rider. Always start with the obvious: check that the saddle fits correctly and get a veterinary surgeon to examine the horse's back, neck and legs. Carry out exercises on the lunge and under saddle to improve the horse's balance and build up muscle strength. If the bucking appears to be caused by overfreshness, make sure the horse is given as much turn-out as possible, and that he is being fed according to the amount of work being done. And, as always, check that he is being ridden correctly, with the rider in balance and not interfering with the horse.

Cold-backed, girth-shy

Horses with this kind of problem are often described as 'cold-backed' when in fact it may have nothing to do with the horse's back. The horse may object to the saddle being put on, in some cases backing up or even rearing. Or he may react to the feel of the girth being tightened; some try to bite, some back up or rear, while others may sag at the knees and go down on the ground.

Above: Exercises on the lunge will help to improve the horse's balance and build up muscle strength.

Above left: Horses should be gradually habituated to the saddle and to being ridden. The saddle is being introduced to this young mare, who has already been allowed to see and sniff at it.

Left: She remains quite relaxed as the saddle is placed carefully on her back.

Top: The girth should be fastened slowly and carefully, and not tightened too suddenly.

Above: It is a good idea to raise the horse's heart rate slightly by means of light exercise such as walking in hand or a little lunging, before actually tacking up.

Possible causes

If the horse objects to the saddle being put on, this may be because he associates the saddle with pain. The saddle may not fit properly and could be causing him pain every time it is put on, or he could simply be remembering pain caused by an ill-fitting saddle in the past. He may have some kind of back problem which is exacerbated every time the saddle is put on, or he may be associating the saddle with unpleasant experiences when he is ridden.

If it is the girth that he objects to, this could be because he dislikes the sensation of having the girth fastened. This is especially likely if the girth is usually tightened suddenly or forcefully; some horses will react to this by actually fainting.

Solution

Ensure that the saddle fits, using the criteria set out in chapter 5 (page 70), and have the horse's back checked by a suitably qualified person. If the problem appears to be an objection to the girth, take extra care when girthing up, tightening the girth tactfully and in small increments. It is a good idea to raise the horse's heart rate slightly by means of light exercise such as walking in hand or a little lunging, before actually tacking up. If the horse continues to object in spite of these precautions, you should ask a veterinary surgeon to check the horse's heart for any irregularities which may be causing a drop in heart rate/blood pressure.

Ducking out of jumps or refusing jumps

A horse who ducks out of jumps or frequently refuses is one of the most frustrating problems for riders who enjoy jumping. Solving it requires tact and understanding on the part of the rider.

Possible causes

Although horses, being natural athletes, are more than capable of jumping quite formidable obstacles, they can sometimes find jumping quite a daunting process. Even though their proprioceptive sense enables them to judge where their hind feet are in relation to the jump, they can make mistakes. If a horse catches his hind feet or his hind cannons on a jump too often, he may become frightened of jumping. The same applies if a horse is overfaced – that is, asked to tackle jumps that are too high and/or too challenging for him. If a jump is beyond a horse's present

Above: Horses can sometimes find jumping quite a daunting process, and refusals are common.

Above right: This horse decided he had had enough jumping for one day and that he did not want to be caught after losing his rider.

Right: Going back to basics can help to solve a number of jumping problems.

capabilities, he may take it awkwardly and land badly, jarring his front legs, neck and spine. Horses can also become sour through being asked to jump too often, especially if they find jumping a stressful experience.

Even if a horse is an experienced jumper, he may have sustained an injury – whether through jumping or from some other cause – which makes him reluctant to jump. Or he may have problems with vision which make it difficult for him to judge the height and spread of a jump.

Prevention

Ensure that the horse has been adequately prepared for jumping through correct basic schooling, including work over trotting poles and raised poles, progressing to basic gridwork. Keep jumping sessions to a minimum; top showjumping riders may pop their horses over jumps only a couple of times a week, concentrating instead on schooling on the flat and riding out for exercise.

Solution

If the horse is frightened of jumping, you will need to go right back to the basics as described previously. Only progress to higher jumps when the horse appears comfortable with what is being asked of him and approaches jumps willingly and without rushing. If the horse still jumps confidently and the refusals/running out appear to be due to sourness, you will need to give him a complete rest from jumping, in some cases for as much as several months. In all cases you should have him examined by a veterinary surgeon to rule out physical pain and problems with vision.

Head tossing

A horse who tosses his head can be very disconcerting for his rider. Fortunately, it need not be a difficult problem to solve.

Possible causes

Head tossing may sometimes be a sign of impatience in a fresh horse. It is far more likely, however, to be caused by pain or discomfort of some kind. Sometimes green horses go through a temporary phase of head tossing while they are growing accustomed to the feel of the bit in their mouths. This usually ceases once the horse becomes habituated to the sensation, which may take only a few days if the rider is sensitive and tactful with the contact. Additionally, when horses are first ridden they quickly become tired, and head tossing may then be a sign of tiredness; this can also occur when more experienced horses are introduced to new exercises which they find difficult and/or taxing. If head tossing occurs regularly and/or for prolonged periods of time, then it may be a symptom of pain in the teeth, from ear abscesses or other infection, or pain occurring in the back and neck.

Poor riding may also be a factor here; an unbalanced, overactive rider will interfere with the horse's ability to use himself properly and this will certainly cause fatigue and, in many cases, pain and injury as well.

Solution

The system adopted by seventeenth- and eighteenth-century horsemen of Europe, of riding a horse in a cavesson (or *caveçon*, as it was known) until his canine teeth had come through at the age of around six, has much to

recommend it. Nowadays increasing numbers of people are returning to this way of thinking and starting young horses under saddle without a bit, progressing to a bit only when the horse is already accustomed to being ridden. Not everyone will feel comfortable with this idea, and for those who do not I would simply advise riding a green horse with a very light contact until he is comfortable with the feel of the bit. Long-reining a horse before he is backed will, if carried out correctly, also help him to accept the bit (see 'Suggested reading' on page 158 for some useful books which cover this much-neglected subject).

Additionally, green horses should initially be ridden for very short periods, sometimes as little as ten minutes. Gradually building up to longer spells of work will help to avoid fatiguing the horse to the point where he starts to throw his head about.

The same applies when introducing more experienced horses to more difficult work; once the horse gives even an approximation of what you want, do not be tempted to persist. Break off the session and give him a rest; that way he will be both physically and psychologically ready for the next training session.

In all cases, have the horse's teeth checked (this should in any case be done regularly) and make sure that the bit fits correctly.

Hollowing

Hollowing is a very common problem, as earlier chapters have shown. In some cases it may be a temporary response, but where it occurs regularly the causes need to be addressed.

Possible causes

Some horses have the kind of conformation that naturally makes them tend to hollow. A ewe-neck (upside down) can make it difficult for a horse to arch his neck in such a way that the 'ring of muscles' can come into play. Still, even such horses can be helped with the kind of exercises described in chapters 6–8. Lack of strength in the neck and back can similarly be addressed by the same exercises. Badly fitting saddles will tend to make horses hollow their backs away from the discomfort, as will riders who are unbalanced and have poor control over their body movements; the latter is perhaps the commonest cause of hollowed backs.

Solution

Where conformation and/or lack of strength are concerned, going back to the basic exercises to build up muscle strength and tone, and improve balance, should help the horse to carry himself in better form. These exercises are best started on the lunge, gradually building up to ridden work as the horse becomes stronger. All tack should be checked to ensure it fits correctly, and as a matter of course you should have the horse's back, neck and legs checked over by a veterinary surgeon. Finally, all riders should take a long hard look at their riding position.

Above: As earlier chapters have shown, hollowing is a very common problem with a number of possible causes. This novice horse is lacking in strength in his neck and back, causing him to hollow; correct schooling will remedy this.

Napping

Some horses become reluctant go forwards when asked. They may not want to leave the yard, and may refuse to progress beyond a certain distance away from the stables. Usually the horse plants himself and refuses to move, but in extreme cases this may lead to running backwards or even rearing.

Possible causes

Such horses may be very insecure and unhappy about moving from an environment where they feel safe. They often become attached to one or more companions to the extent that they grow distressed and even hysterical on being separated from these companions, even for a short time.

Solution

Slowly and carefully habituate the horse to being separated from his companions and the safety of familiar ground. Take him to a distance just before you know he usually becomes upset, and stop there. Reward him for going that far, then return him to where he feels safe. Once you can do this without him showing any signs of stress, you can gradually start to increase the distance – always stopping before he becomes distressed. As soon as he will go a little further without getting upset, reward him and take him back to the stables or his field. In this way you can keep increasing his comfort zone, until eventually he is happy to go further and further without panicking.

   (See also under 'Refusing or reluctance to go forwards', page 147.)

Not standing still to be mounted

Many riders are extremely frustrated and annoyed by their horse's habit of moving off as soon as they have got their left foot in the stirrup. The resulting ineffectual hopping about is not only undignified, but could also be dangerous if the rider then falls backwards onto a hard surface such as a concrete yard.

Possible causes

One possible cause is that the horse has at some time been prodded in the side when the rider is mounting. If this happens once or twice it may not leave a lasting impression, but if it has been a regular occurrence the horse will probably have come to regard being mounted as an unpleasant experience to be avoided if possible. It may even be that the rider's toe has inadvertently set off a reflex response in the horse which results in him moving forwards – if we think about the action of the rider's leg at or just behind the girth, we can see how likely this possibility is.

   Another factor that may make the horse see being

Opposite top: Many horses get into the habit of moving off as the rider starts to mount. This rider is taking great care not to dig her toes into the horse's side, but the habit is too deeply ingrained and he continues to walk off as she is mounting.

Opposite middle: The first step in retraining is to ask the horse to stand still next to the mounting block.

Opposite bottom: When the horse is standing quietly, he should be rewarded. This horse is being given a small amount of his favourite food.

Above: Eventually, the rider tries preparing to mount. It will take some time to retrain this horse, but at the time of writing he was making good progress.

mounted as an unpleasant experience is having the saddle pulled out of position when the rider mounts. This can be very uncomfortable or even painful for the horse.

One explanation that is sometimes put forward is that the horse tries to avoid being mounted because he thinks of the rider as a possible predator. As we saw under 'Bucking', however, it is actually very unlikely that horses think of

riders in this way. The memory of pain and discomfort are very much more likely as possible causes.

Solution

Where moving off before the rider has become settled in the saddle has become a habit, the horse will have to be retrained using positive reinforcement. You will need an assistant to help you with this, and you will need to use a mounting block of some kind.

- Lead the horse up to the mounting block and stand on the block yourself. It does not matter if the horse stands askew – we just want him to stand quietly for a few seconds. Once he has complied, reward him as described in chapter 4. If he moves forwards, bring him back into position and start again. If he swings round to face you, get your assistant to push him gently back into position parallel to the mounting block. He will soon understand that standing still parallel to the block gets him the reward. Gradually increase the amount of time you ask him to stand still until you can get him to stand quietly for several minutes.
- Once he will stand without moving forwards or swinging round/away from the block, try preparing to mount. If the horse continues to stand still, reward him and end the lesson. Repeat this several times (spread over a number of sessions) until he reliably stands still every time you go to mount from the block.
- Finally, with your assistant standing on the other side of the horse (but not holding him) in case he moves, try putting your foot in the stirrup, swing your leg over the horse's back and settle gently into the saddle. If he moves, try again; if he continues to stand still, reward him. Repeat this procedure over a number of sessions and eventually you will have a horse who stands still instead of moving off every time you go to mount.

Wherever possible, use a mounting block of some kind (or a fence, large rock, or anything else handy) or get someone to give you a leg up. If you must mount from the ground, take care not to dig your toe in the horse's side; rather than grasp the cantle as so many people do, place your right hand on the far side of the saddle's seat and use your hand to lever yourself up into the saddle. This will help to prevent the saddle being pulled to one side.

Opening mouth; tongue over the bit/lolling out to the side

This is a common problem and especially frustrating for riders who wish to compete in dressage, as they will lose marks if their horse opens his mouth to any significant degree. (This action should not be confused with the soft 'mouthing' of the bit which is necessary for the horse to maintain a moist mouth and to prevent tension from stiffening the muscles of the neck.)

Above: *Opening the mouth may be caused by discomfort in the mouth itself, tension in the back and neck, or in some cases actual injury to the neck.*

Possible causes

If the horse is uncomfortable in his mouth and/or neck, he will try to relieve the discomfort in any way he can – in this case by retracting/lolling his tongue. The cause may be an ill-fitting or badly adjusted bit, harsh, pulling hands, tension in the back and neck caused by rider imbalance, or in some cases actual injury to the neck.

Solution

Have the horse examined by a veterinary surgeon to eliminate neck injury/pain from the teeth and jaw as possible causes. Check the fit of the bit, bridle and saddle as advised in chapter 5, and of course take a long hard look at your position in the saddle and use of the aids.

Pulling

Some horses lean heavily on the bit and bear down on the rider's hand, in extreme cases threatening to pull the rider out of the saddle.

Possible causes

Some horses try to seek relief from bit discomfort by pulling because the resulting pressure numbs the affected area, just as humans suffering from toothache will press a finger against the gum near the offending tooth in an attempt to block the pain. In other cases the horse may be weak in the back and neck, and may be trying to use the rider's hands as a 'fifth leg'. Or the rider may be taking too hard a contact, and the horse is attempting to dislodge the rider so as to relieve the pressure. An unbalanced rider seat may have the same effect.

Solution

There is a saying that it takes two to pull, and this is perfectly correct. Horses can only pull against the rider if the latter allows them to do so. In all cases, action should be taken as for horses who open the mouth; once pain from the teeth and/or bit has been eliminated, schooling exercises as described in chapters 6–8 can commence, to build up strength in the relevant muscles of the neck and back. If the horse persists in trying to dislodge the rider, all the latter has to do is firm up his or her position and resist passively. The horse will soon realize that he is not getting anywhere, and as he gains in strength and self-carriage he will no longer feel the need to prop himself up on the rider's hand.

Above: American classical trainer Paul Belasik likes to demonstrate how to deal with a pulling horse by showing how the rider can resist the pull. Here, Belasik takes the part of the pulling horse by passing a lunge line around the rider's body; the rider must then resist the pull by firming up the back and abdominal muscles.

Rearing

This is one of the most frightening, as well as dangerous, of resistances under saddle. A confirmed rearer can be very difficult to retrain, and such horses are best left to people with sufficient experience to deal with them sympathetically yet with the necessary firmness. Horses who rear only occasionally can still be very alarming, and this is a problem that needs to be dealt with quickly if it is not to become a habit.

Possible causes

As with so many problems under saddle, rearing often has its roots in pain, usually in the neck and back, but on occasion in the limbs as well. Sometimes freshness can be a cause: the horse wants to have a fling, but is restrained by the rider, so he rears in protest; or he may simply be unwilling to go forwards.

Solution

See under 'Bucking' and also under 'Refusing or reluctance to go forwards'.

Refusing or reluctance to go forwards

This is one of the most common and frustrating of the many problems experienced by riders. The rider whose horse does not go forwards has to work so hard just to keep him going that, instead of being an enjoyable experience, riding becomes an exhausting battle. Some riders simply become discouraged and ride less and less as a result, while others may become so annoyed and frustrated that they take these frustrations out on the horse.

Lack of forward movement can also physically injure the horse, as a horse who is not using himself properly will not develop the proper muscles to carry a rider without physical damage.

Above: Rearing is a very dangerous and frightening behaviour.

Riders and trainers often regard a horse's refusal to move forwards freely as a sign of laziness, stubbornness and a general unwillingness to co-operate. There are many possible causes of this lack of co-operation, however, and as always we must investigate them thoroughly and eliminate the cause before we attempt a cure.

Possible causes

Pain

Reluctance to move forwards may be caused by pain occurring almost anywhere in the body, and as with most problems this possibility must always be thoroughly investigated.

Lack of energy

Some horses may simply be lacking sufficient energy to carry a rider.

Fear of loss of balance

Horses who have just been started under saddle, or those who are recovering from an injury, may be reluctant to move forwards because they fear a loss of balance under the rider's weight. This is one of the commonest reasons why horses may 'act up' when first ridden.

Lack of strength

If the horse has not been adequately prepared for ridden work, or has not been in regular work, he may simply not have sufficient strength to carry a rider efficiently.

Lack of motivation

Many people believe that horses cannot become bored as they do not have sufficiently complex mental processes. There is ample evidence from recent research that this is not the case, and that horses are in fact capable of a certain degree of reasoning and abstract thought.

Solution

Have the horse's back, neck and legs checked by a veterinary surgeon and get a properly qualified equine dentist to examine his teeth, as the horse may be hanging back because he is trying to avoid contact with the bit. An equine dentist will also be able to look at the size and shape of the horse's mouth and check to see whether the bit fits properly. The horse's tack should also be checked to ensure that it fits correctly, because ill-fitting tack is a common cause of reluctance to move forwards.

If the cause is a lack of energy, the solution may be a simple matter of adjusting the amount/type of the horse's feed. As a lack of energy may be a sign of some underlying health problem, however, this should always be discussed with the vet at the same time as the horse is examined for possible causes of pain.

Where loss of balance appears to be the cause, the rider must ensure their position in the saddle is correct and that they sit as still as possible, because an unbalanced rider who bumps around in the saddle will make the horse feel even more 'wobbly' and reluctant to move.

After all the necessary checks have been carried out to eliminate pain as a cause, the horse should first of all be taken back to basics on the lunge in order to build up his muscle strength and tone, and improve his balance. Once the horse is moving forwards freely on the lunge, his muscles have become more toned and he can stay on a circle without either hanging back or rushing to regain his balance, ridden exercises may be started which will help to establish and maintain forward movement and impulsion (see chapters 6–8).

Horses need mental stimulation, and some horses may simply 'switch off' when being worked in an arena or other enclosed space. The same horses may become much more animated and forward-going when ridden out in the country or on the road because they find the change of scenery exciting and even entertaining. Other horses may be quite happy to work in an arena as long as the work is varied and interesting, and they are challenged by their work without being overtaxed. By varying the type and location of their work, and ensuring they are rewarded when they have done well, such horses are encouraged by their riders to enjoy their work and even look forward to it.

Resistance to the leg

Some horses seem 'dead to the leg' because they do not respond to anything but a kick, and may even cease to respond to that.

Possible causes

As we saw in chapter 4, squeezing the horse's sides will effectively block the nerve impulses which stimulate the muscles. Repeated thumping of the horse's sides will have the same effect; in addition, the horse will become habituated to the meaningless sensation and will effectively 'switch off' to the leg aids.

Solution

Correct use of the legs as described in chapters 3 and 4.

Spookiness

The horse who persistently spooks (shies), often for no apparent reason, can make riding a frustrating and sometimes frightening experience.

Possible causes

One of the commonest causes of spookiness is freshness, whether from lack of exercise or from overfeeding. Sometimes horses become spooky because they sense that the rider is nervous. Not knowing the reason for this nervousness (which might have any number of causes), the horse may start to think that something in the environment is causing the rider to feel alarm. He will then start looking for things at which to spook. Sudden movements in the horse's peripheral field of vision may disturb him; horses are very good at detecting movement, but may not always be able to see very clearly what it is that is moving. Their natural inclination is to get away from anything strange, so a sudden shy may be the result.

Solution

Always observe the golden rule of feeding according to the work being done, and ensure the horse is allowed plenty of turn-out time, preferably with congenial companions. The procedures described in chapter 6 will help to calm and relax him and gain his attention before starting ridden work. If you are usually nervous, or his shying is making you nervous with anticipation, improving your own riding so that you feel more secure in the saddle will help you to feel safer and less apprehensive. There are a number of disciplines, such as yoga, which will help you to combat nervousness (see 'Useful contacts' on page 155 for more details.

If the shying is very severe and frequent, and especially if it always occurs when the horse is being ridden in one particular direction, problems with vision may be the cause. Arrange for a veterinary surgeon to examine the horse, either to eliminate or to confirm this possibility.

Refusal to stop

Along with the horse who will not go forwards, the horse who will not stop is one of the commonest problems faced by riders. Some horses are difficult to stop only during fast work; others are difficult to stop in any gait, even from a slow walk.

Possible causes

The horse who is difficult to stop from a faster gait may simply have become excited. As always, make sure that he is not being fed too much for the amount of work he is doing, and that he has sufficient turn-out time to get rid of excess energy. Horses who feel themselves out of balance will often go faster because loss of balance matters less at faster paces.

Horses who will not slow down or stop in slower gaits may also be feeling unbalanced, or may be unsure how to respond to confusing rider signals.

Solution

Go back to basics in a safe, enclosed space, making sure that the horse is responsive in slower gaits before asking for canter. When you do take him to canter, ask for only half a circuit of the schooling area to begin with (or less if you feel he is starting to get excited). Gradually build up to longer spells of canter in the enclosed area, with lots of transitions from one gait to another and back again, and do not canter in wide open spaces until you are sure the horse will respond to your requests to slow down. The same applies to cantering and galloping in company; nothing excites horses more than other horses galloping. Where the problem occurs in slower gaits, schooling exercises with lots of transitions will help. And, as always, ensure that your own riding position and use of the aids are not confusing the horse or unbalancing him.

Conclusion

THUS WROTE one of the greatest horsemen of the twentieth century. He knew that, in riding and training horses, we can never know all there is to know. He could never say, as some trainers do, 'Follow my method, and you will learn all you need to know about riding and

training horses' because he knew that there is no such method, no 'one-size-fits-all' philosophy that apples to every horse. Trainers can give us ready-made recipes for success, but that is all they are: recipes. If we do not understand how the various components work, we have no option but to follow the recipe rigidly. If something goes wrong – say, we forget one of the ingredients or misunderstand the instructions – we have nothing to fall back on. We do not know how to get ourselves – and our horses – out of the resulting mess.

If instead of looking for recipes and quick fixes, however, we take the trouble to understand how a horse's body works and how the horse and his rider interact, we have the foundation for a set of training principles which will enable us to devise our own training strategies. We can create – and adapt – these training strategies to suit the individual horse and his individual circumstances. This is what the great classical horsemen have done for centuries: they studied the anatomy of horses, how they move, how they respond to different exercises, how they react to what a

Left: *Proper schooling is essential, especially for naturally exuberant horses such as Lusitano mare Queijada, seen here with Sylvia Loch, who is able to channel the mare's energy into productive work.*

Right: *Even if all a rider wants to do is ride out, a well-schooled horse will make this a much safer and more pleasurable experience. These two horses are stable-mates and always enjoy a hack out together.*

rider does on their backs, and so on. The principles they worked out as a result of these studies have been added to, and in some cases improved, by other great horsemen and women. These principles continue to be used, wherever good horsemanship is practised, because they *work*.

We have seen that proper schooling is essential if we are to keep our horses sound and athletic throughout their working lives; this applies even if all we want to do is ride out in the countryside and have fun. Schooling requires self-discipline and commitment, but it need not be a chore. If we approach it in the right frame of mind, it can be an absorbing and rewarding experience.

We have also seen how the horse's body works in such a way that we can make use of his 'sixth sense' – his proprioceptive sense – in riding and training him. Neither we nor the horse need to learn a complex set of instructions. Provided we learn how to use our bodies, and sit correctly on the horse's back, we can make use of his natural responses, not only to get him to do what we want him to do, but also to enhance his performance under saddle. We can use the aids to do what aids are supposed to do: not merely tell the horse what we want him to do, but actively *help* him to comply.

Using our knowledge of how the horse's body works, we will be able to see – and feel – whether he is working correctly. An understanding of the horse–rider interaction enables us to solve problems caused by our own asymmetries and imbalances, instead of – as so often happens – blaming the horse and seeking remedies that either will have limited success or cannot work at all because they are addressing the wrong causes.

Through the medium of the training exercises themselves, we can restore a horse's athletic performance to something near what it was before we burdened him with a saddle, a bridle, a bit and – most restrictive of all – the weight of a rider. By understanding what each exercise does, we can tailor our exercise programmes to the individual horse's needs, by emphasizing those exercises which will enhance the horse's strengths and remedy any weaknesses. By incorporating these exercises into schooling patterns, we will be able to give our training sessions a structure with specific aims.

Finally, the greater our understanding of all these things, the better our chances of preventing problems will be, and the more versatile a tool kit we will have in our possession for dealing with problems when they do arise.

Good horsemanship takes time and effort to achieve, but the rewards – in terms of increased riding skills, better performance on the part of our horses, and greater harmony between horse and rider – are incalculable.

Left: *The ultimate goal of schooling is harmony between horse and rider.*

Useful contacts and organizations

All information is correct at the time of going to press.

The Alexander Technique

According to the official website, 'The Alexander Technique is a method that works to change (movement) habits in our everyday activities. It is a simple and practical method for improving ease and freedom of movement, balance, support and co-ordination. The technique teaches the use of the appropriate amount of effort for a particular activity, giving you more energy for all your activities. It is not a series of treatments or exercises, but rather a re-education of the mind and body. The Alexander Technique is a method which helps a person discover a new balance in the body by releasing unnecessary tension. It can be applied to sitting, lying down, standing, walking, lifting, and other daily activities …'

This extremely informative website can be found at **www.alexandertechnique.com**. On the website you can find information about the Alexander Technique and details of Alexander teachers worldwide.

Body Control Pilates

Body Control Pilates exercises are based on the classical Pilates exercises devised by the founder, Joseph Pilates. According to the Body Control Pilates website, central to the method is 'awareness of your own body', and each and every exercise is built around Pilates' eight basic principles:

- relaxation
- concentration
- co-ordination
- centring
- alignment
- breathing
- stamina
- flowing movements

Body Control Pilates
35 Little Russell Street
London WC1A 2HH
United Kingdom
Tel: + 44 + 20 7636 8900
Fax: + 44 + 20 7636 8898
E-mail: info@bodycontrol.co.uk

The website can be found at
www.bodycontrol.co.uk/information.html
From there you can find a link to information about an international network of instructors:
www.bodycontrol.co.uk/InternationalIndex.html

The Classical Riding Club

The Classical Riding Club was started in 1995 by internationally renowned trainer, writer and lecturer Sylvia Loch, as a means of bringing together like-minded people who were interested in a more philosophical approach to riding which puts the happiness and wellbeing of the horse above all else. The Classical Riding Club's membership is truly international and includes people with widely differing equestrian backgrounds and levels of ability.

The Classical Riding Club
Eden Hall
Kelso
Roxburghshire TD5 7QD
United Kingdom
Fax: + 44 1890 830667
E-mail: crc@classicalriding.co.uk
Website: www.classicalriding.co.uk

Yoga

For information about yoga teachers worldwide, contact the International Yoga Federation.

E-mail: fiy@yoganet.org
Website: www.internationalyogafederation.net

National equestrian federations

The national equestrian federations listed below are members of the Fédération Equestre Internationale (FEI). They can provide advice about riding schools, competition rules and instructors in your area.

Australia

Equestrian Federation of Australia
PO Box 673
Sydney Markets
NSW 2129
Australia
Tel: + 61 2 8762 7777
Fax: + 61 2 9763 2466
Website: www.efanational.com

Austria

Bundesfachverband für Reiten und Fahren in Österreich
Geiselbergstrasse 26-32/512
1110 Wien
Austria
Tel: + 43 1 7499261
Fax: + 43 1 7499261-91
Website: www.fena.at

Belgium

Fédération Royale Belge des Sports Equestres
Avenue Hooba de Strooper 156
1020 Bruxelles
Belgium
Tel: + 32 2 478 5056
Fax: + 32 + 2 478 1126
Website: www.equibel.be

Denmark

Dansk Ride Forbund
Idraettens Hus
Brøndby Stadion 20
2605 Brøndby
Denmark
Tel: + 45 43 26 28 28
Fax: + 45 43 26 28 12
Website: www.rideforbund.dk

France

Fédération Française d'Équitation
81 avenue Edouard Vaillant
92517 Boulogne cedex
Tel: + 33 1 58 17 58 22
Fax: + 33 1 58 17 58 19
Website: www.ffe.com

Germany

Deutsche Reiterliche Vereinigung
Freiherr-von-Langen-Strasse 13
48231 Warendorf
Germany
Tel: + 49 2581 63620
Fax: + 49 2581 62144
Website: www.pferd-aktuell.de

Ireland

Equestrian Federation of Ireland
Willow House
Millennium Park
Osberstown
Naas, Co. Kildare
Ireland
Tel: + 353 45 854040
Fax: + 353 45 854041 or 854042
Website: www.horsesport.ie

Italy

Federazione Italiana Sport Equestri

Viale Tiziano 74-76

Rome 00196

Italy

Tel: + 39 6 36858105

Fax: + 39 6 32 33 772

Website: www.fise.it

Luxembourg

Fédération Luxembourgeoise des Sports Equestres

3, route d'Arlon

L-8009 Strassen

Tel: +352 48 49 99

Fax: +352 48 50 39

Website: www.flse.lu

Monaco

Fédération Equestre de la Principauté de Monaco

Villa Gardenia, 3 Avenue Saint Michel

Monte Carlo 98000

Tel: + 377 93 50 80 54

Fax: + 377 93 50 80 56

Website: www.federation-equestre.mc

The Netherlands

Koninklijke Nederlandse Hippische Sportfederatie

(Royal Dutch Equestrian Federation)

De Beek 125

3852 PL Ermelo

The Netherlands

Tel: + 31 577 40 82 00

Fax: + 31 577 40 17 25

Website: www. knhs.nl

New Zealand

Equestrian Sports New Zealand

PO Box 6146

Wellington

New Zealand

Tel: + 64 4 499 8994

Fax: + 64 4 499 2899

Website: www.nzequestrian.org.nz

Norway

Norges Rytterforbund

Servicebox 1Ullevål Stadium

0840 Oslo

Norway

Tel: + 47 21 02 96 50

Fax: + 47 21 02 96 51

Website: www.rytter.no

Portugal

Federação Equestre Portuguesa

Avenida Manuel da Maia, 26 – 4° Dt°

1000-201 Lisbon

Portugal

Tel: + 35 21 847 8774

Fax: + 35 21 847 4582

Website: www.fep.pt

South Africa

South African National Equestrian Federation

PO Box 30875

Kyalami 1684

Gauteng

South Africa

Tel: + 27 11 468 3236 or 468 3237

Fax: + 27 11 468 3238

Website: www.horsesport.org.za

Spain

Real Federación Hípica Española

C/Monte Esquinza, n° 28 – 3°

28010 – Madrid

Spain

Tel: +34 91 436 42 00

Fax: + 34 91 575 07 70 or 575 08 44

Website: www.refhe.com

Sweden

Svenska Ridsportförbundet

Ridsportens hus

Strömsholm

734 94 Strömsholm

Sweden

Tel: + 46 220 456 00

Fax: + 46 220 456 70

Website: www.ridsport.se

Switzerland

Fédération Suisse des Sports Equestres/Schweizerischer

Verban für Pferdesport

CH-3000 Bern 22

Box 726, Papiermühlestrasse 40H

Switzerland

Tel: + 41 31 335 43 43

Fax: + 41 31 335 43 57 or 335 43 58

Website: www.svps-fsse.ch

United Kingdom

British Equestrian Federation

National Agricultural Centre

Stoneleigh Park, Kenilworth

Warwickshire CV8 2RH

United Kingdom

Tel: + 44 2476 698871

Fax: + 44 2476 696484

Website: www.bef.co.uk

United States of America

United States Equestrian Federation (formerly the
American Horse Shows Association)

4047 Iron Works Parkway

Lexington, KY 40511

USA

Tel: + 1 859 258 2472

Fax: +1 859 231 6662

Website: www.usef.org

International equestrian federation

Fédération Equestre Internationale (FEI)

Avenue Mon Repos 24

1005 Lausanne

Switzerland

Tel: + 41 21 310 47 47

Fax: + 41 21 310 47 60

Website: www.horsesport.org

Suggested reading

Albrecht, Brigadier General Kurt (1993), *Principles of Dressage* (London: J. A. Allen).

Bennett, Dr Deb (1994), 'True collection', *Equus*, no. 198, April 1994.

Bennett, Dr Deb (1998), *Conquerors: The Roots of New World Horsemanship* (Solvang, California: Amigo Publications).

Blignault, Karin (1997), *Successful Schooling* (London: J. A. Allen).

Bürger, Udo (1999), *The Way to Perfect Horsemanship*, rev. edn, trans. Nicole Bartle, Allen's Classic (London: J. A. Allen).

de Kunffy, Charles (1992), *The Athletic Development of the Dressage Horse: Manege Patterns* (New York: Howell Book House).

de Kunffy, Charles (1993), *The Ethics and Passions of Dressage* (Middletown, Md: Half Halt Press).

Edwards, Elwyn Hartley (2004), *The Complete Book of Bits and Bitting* (Newton Abbot: David & Charles).

Herbermann, Erik F. (1999), *Dressage Formula* (London: J. A. Allen).

Karl, Philippe (2003), *Long Reining: The Saumur Method* (Vermont: Trafalgar Square Publishing).

Klimke, Ingrid & Reiner (2000), *Cavalletti: Schooling of Horse and Rider over Ground Rails*, rev. edn (London: J. A. Allen).

Loch, Sylvia (1988), *The Classical Seat: A Guide for the Everyday Rider* (London: Unwin Hyman in association with *Horse and Rider*).

Loch, Sylvia (1997), *The Classical Rider: Being at One with Your Horse* (London: J. A. Allen).

Loch, Sylvia (2000), *Dressage in Lightness: Speaking the Horse's Language* (London: J. A. Allen).

Oliveira, Nuno (1976), *Reflections on Equestrian Art*, trans. Phyllis Field (London: J. A. Allen).

Pryor, Karen (1999), *Don't Shoot the Dog!: The New Art of Teaching and Training*, rev. edn (New York: Bantam Books).

Seunig, Waldemar (2003), *Horsemanship: A Comprehensive Book on Training the Horse and Its Rider*, tr. Leonard Mins, Allen Classic Series, (London: J.A. Allen; originally published in New York: Doubleday, 1956).

Sivewright, Molly (1999), *Thinking Riding* (Book 1) (London: J. A. Allen).

Sivewright, Molly (1999), *Thinking Riding: In Good Form* (Book 2) (London: J. A. Allen).

Stanier, Sylvia (1993), *The Art of Lungeing*, rev. edn (London: J. A. Allen).

Stanier, Sylvia (1995), *The Art of Long Reining*, rev. edn (London: J. A. Allen).

Swift, Sally (1985), *Centered Riding* (New York: St Martin's/Marek).

van Laun, Richenda, & Sylvia Loch (2000), *Flexibility and Fitness for Riders*, Allen Photographic Guides (London: J. A. Allen).

Wyche, Sara (1998), *Understanding the Horse's Back* (Marlborough: Crowood Press).

Wyche, Sara (2004), *The Anatomy of Riding* (Marlborough: Crowood Press).

Index

Credits and acknowledgements

All photography by Lesley Skipper, with the exception of those supplied by the following photographers and/or agencies (copyright rests with these individuals and/or their agencies): Bob Langrish: pages 14, 37, 133 (both), 136, 137 and 147.

New Holland Publishers would like to thank Penny Brown for the index.